The

HANDBOOK

of

PRACTICAL RESILIENCE

How to survive in the 21st century

Elizabeth J Walker

Published by New Generation Publishing in 2020

This is a Second Edition
Previously released in 2015 as 'The Resilience Handbook – how to survive in the 21st Century'
The Second Edition is revised and has extra content

ISBN 978-1-80031-919-6

www.newgeneration-publishing.com
New Generation Publishing

This is a Second Edition.

This edition is dedicated to the legendary
Mr Mario Teo and his
amazing team

Contents

individuals studying alone, or for working in a group.

Preface

The Handbook of Practical Resilience is a guide to how the interacting complexities of modern times can be managed to create a future with less energy use but a better quality of life.

Resources are being depleted across the globe, while demand for them rises. Nations will have to move towards greater self-sufficiency as their trading partners need to keep more for their own use.

Our current lifestyle in Britain is dangerously dependent on non-renewable energy sources, such as fossil fuels and nuclear power. Without substantial imports of food, we cannot support 70 million people on this island.

Yet only seventy years ago, just after the all-out self-sufficiency campaigns of the Second World War, we could have nearly fed our entire population. Craftspeople ran small businesses in every High Street where items could be bought or repaired. Town centre market gardens thrived.

We could have built on this resilience to become a nation self-sufficient in essentials, but chose instead to pursue the path of consumerism. Now, the High Street is occupied by chain stores who remove money from your local area as soon as it passes over their counters. The market gardens are car parks and the population has nearly doubled.

Environmentalists argue with politicians, scientists with religious leaders, and year after year nothing is done. The endless economic growth promised seems to have turned cancerous. Resource wars are flaring up.

However serious the situation is, however impossible a solution seems, we arrived here slowly, one piece of shopping at a time. We need to take back our power and make new choices. While we still have access to fossil fuel energy, we can use it to rebuild a resilient culture. There's no time to lose.

This Handbook outlines how to proceed in an immediate and realistic way. Accessible ground level strategies are combined in the move towards practical resilience, where every positive effort counts.

Chapter One

Resilience – what does it mean?

It's not easy to explain or define 'resilience'. Simply described, it is the ability to cope well with change. It can be applied to materials, ecosystems or entire planets, but here we are dealing with resilience in people, in communities and in cultures.

Resilience is a concept with depth, one that exists and develops through time, like loyalty, honesty and common sense. It implies a knowledge of what is valuable, what must continue, where to strive to repair and regenerate, what should not be discarded.

Resilience is often associated with sustainability. The two concepts are closely linked. An unsustainable practice is doomed to eventual failure, so it is not resilient. Sustainability tends to start at the luxury end of the market and work downwards while resilience focuses on need and works upwards.

Sustainability asks "could you involve less air miles when choosing which food to buy?" Resilience asks less comfortable questions such as "how much food can you access within walking distance of your home?"

In this country we are used to – dependent on – a highly organised infrastructure to deliver all that we require, from anywhere in the world. In order to move towards greater resilience, we need to source our essential goods and services closer to home. We need to revitalise our local economies, producing more power and food so we are less vulnerable to global events.

A resilient community needs to be able to cope with the impact of a disaster. If you are on the sharp end of it, if your area is the one which is actually flooded, severely damaged or contaminated, presenting a united front will secure more help and ensure it is deployed to best effect. If the actual problem happens elsewhere, your community could have to deal with major disruption of essential services.

If large cities are badly affected, nearby rural areas may have to fend for themselves before official help arrives.

"Local emergency responders will always have to prioritise those in greatest need during an emergency, focusing their efforts where life is in danger. There will be times when individuals and communities are affected by an emergency but are not in any immediate danger and will have to look after themselves and each other for a period until any necessary external assistance can be provided. Communities will need to work together, and with service providers, to determine how they recover from an emergency."
From the 'Strategic National Framework on Community Resilience' Cabinet Office (March 2011).

If we were suddenly thrown on our own resources by some disaster - in our country or in a foreign land which happens to control a lot of our energy or food supplies – we'd be struggling to know where to start.

We need to educate ourselves and reform our communities so that we could work together effectively in difficult times. Emergency off-grid power, equipment for evacuation centres, fresh food to add to tinned or dried supplies, a local well or spring prepared for use, a temporary waste disposal strategy – none of this can be produced overnight, nor by a single person. It needs to be prepared in advance.

Community resilience is defined as "Communities and individuals harnessing local resources and expertise to help themselves in an emergency, in a way that complements the response of the emergency services"

Civil Protection Lexicon (2010)

Although available strategies depend on the particular situation, resilient individuals and communities know how to make maximum use of whatever is to hand. Resilience may be tested by circumstance but is not controlled by it.

A resilient individual can survive. Within a resilient community, they can thrive.

Resilience is all about response to change. It is the ability to absorb disturbances and incorporate new factors while keeping a core identity intact and functional.

Change can come in many forms. The fossil fuel bonanza of recent centuries has enabled people to become detached from each other and pursue their individual desires without reference to local resources or communities. As a consequence, these communities and resources are no longer available to support us through the next major change as this abundant – but not renewable – fuel begins to become scarcer.

'Peak Oil' is the term used to describe the point where new fossil fuel discoveries no longer compensate for the steadily decreasing production of existing oil fields and coal mines. Many people believe we have already reached this point. Others consider that we should abandon the use of fossil fuels regardless, due to their impact on the global climate.

We need to come to terms with the end of the cheap energy to which we have become accustomed. Rather than desperately clinging to an unsustainable and energy hungry way of life, we could take a positive attitude to this change. Managing it with care, we could achieve a more relaxed and community centred culture, retaining useful labour saving technology and trading quality goods for our overseas luxuries.

For those who haven't encountered it yet, Transition provides a great deal of support for this process.

The Transition Movement

With the price of fuel, you may not feel that oil is cheap in any real sense, but for operating machinery, running factories and processing other natural resources, the power of fossil fuel is incredible compared to that of manual labour. After centuries of technological growth, we are finally arriving at the point where advanced machine design and renewable energy sources can replace the use of oil, and just in time.

The infrastructure and, to some extent, the lifestyle created around fossil fuels needs to change. The Transition network is dedicated to supporting this process, using strategies initially derived from the philosophy of permanent agriculture, or 'permaculture'.

Totnes, in Devon, became the first 'Transition Town' in 2006. Rob Hopkins, the driving force behind this achievement, published 'The Transition Handbook' in 2008, which outlines the arguments behind an 'energy descent' scenario and encourages community involvement in positive solutions. Many other towns have now adopted Transition Initiatives and the movement has spread globally.

A Transition Initiative looks at forming an Energy Descent Action Plan for their area, exploring how local resources can be used in a more sustainable model and outlining the path of this transition. As life with lower energy consumption is inevitable, it is best to plan for it and Transition maintains that the increase in quality of life will more than compensate for any inconvenience.

Transition is 'an invitation to join the hundreds of communities around the world who are taking the steps towards making a nourishing and abundant future a reality' (Rob Hopkins, 'The Transition Handbook')

Resilience is a key feature of a Transition policy.

"Contingency planning is essential when difficulties and serious challenges face society. While the main mobilisation plan will be at national and regional level, locally a strong plan can help mitigate the worst impacts of difficulties likely to be experienced due to sudden energy shortages and climate change. In conjunction with community representatives, local leaders need to agree a clear set of priorities and make preparations in the event of any national emergency due to sudden extreme changes in weather, sea level or energy cuts." (Jacqi Hodgson and Rob Hopkins, 'Transition in Action')

One of the challenges in implementing an Energy Descent Action Plan is to assess the current situation. There are so many factors bound up in our use of energy – not just heating and lighting but cheap imported food, car use, plastic goods, waste – that it is difficult to consider them all.

There is also a great variation in awareness and constructive action. Some will walk miles to avoid supermarket shopping; others think they are radical if they grow their own kitchen herbs. Both are right of course. Much depends on your situation and the opportunities available.

When teaching or learning resilience, the starting point could be very different for each person or group. An absolute goal and an easily described path may not be the most workable option.

Explaining how rinsing out your plastic bottles would help you survive a meteor strike on London became too involved and confusing, so our resilience group reinvented the wheel.

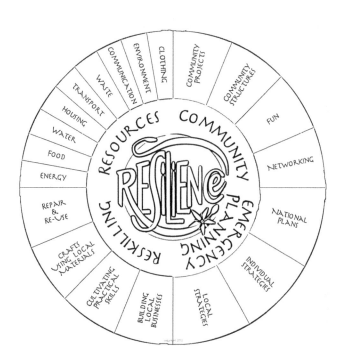

Chapter Two

The Resilience Wheel

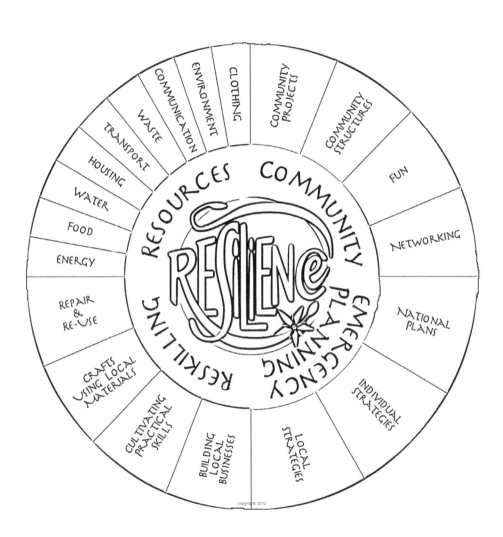

The Resilience Wheel displays the interaction of important factors that must be addressed in achieving resilience. The centre represents you. Visualise yourself as gazing out from this centre, looking at a landscape which surrounds you. Within this landscape are the resources you use in daily life, the people you interact with, your possessions and skills, situations you may encounter.

This landscape is relevant to you personally.

You can change it, gradually making it more resilient. Change of this sort involves many interlocking factors, all of which have to be balanced in order to move together. Hence the image of the Wheel.

There are twenty sections in the Resilience Wheel, arranged in four quadrants. These cover the factors you cannot neglect when cultivating personal, practical resilience.
The **Resources quadrant** contains nine sections – energy, food, water, housing, transport, waste, communication, clothing, and the environment.
The **Reskilling quadrant** has four sections – re-use and repair, practical skills, local materials, and local businesses.
The **Community quadrant** also has four sections – community projects, community structures, networking, and fun.
The final quadrant, **Emergency Planning**, has three sections – individual strategies, local strategies, and national plans.

Positive input into any one section or group of sections increases resilience as a whole.

Resilience looks to local solutions for all the necessities of life. All parts of the Wheel move forward together. However, the problem with interdependent elements is that progress in any one section can eventually be stalled through lack of application in another. Viewing resilience as a unified concept helps you to identify barriers and see where issues need to be addressed.

Start in the **Reskilling quadrant**, for example. You can learn to make your own willow baskets, you can sell them to your friends, you can harvest and process your own willow. All this will take time and eventually you will need to sell enough baskets to supply most of your other needs, or do something else. To move forward with the basket making, you will need to grow a local business, for which the support of a community is important in changing consumer habits.

You've started in the **Practical Skills** section, then included **Local Materials** and **Local Businesses.** If you're expanding your basket making to the stage where it could earn you a living, you'll need to engage with the **Community** quadrant.

Maybe you'd like to grow willow. Could you initiate a **Community Project** to buy land, perhaps organise grant funding through the **Environment** section in the **Resources** quadrant? Willow thrives in wet conditions and is a very useful resource for **Emergency Planning** where flood water needs to be retained in managed areas, or slopes and banks stabilised. It also cleans the soil of some heavy metals and other toxins, ready to grow food crops.

Basket weaving may not be your thing. Let's start somewhere else. How do you get to work?

You'll be using **Transport**. Walking is ideal, but rarely possible especially in rural areas. Cycling is good for longer distances, but here we run into safety issues. For many people, the cycle ride to work is simply too dangerous to be a good option. If this is so, unless you can use public transport, your progress in this section will be limited.

How can you overcome this? Look at the rest of the Resilience Wheel for ideas.

The danger is caused by other road users, people using motorised transport. Perhaps you need **Communication** to persuade them to engage with a solution? Look at the **Community** quadrant. You could form an association, a **Community Structure** to lobby for improved road safety. **Networking** will show you that there are already groups working on this. Can they help you? Meanwhile, keep practising on your bike even if you have to load it into your car and drive it to somewhere safe!

In the event of a major disruption to our fuel supplies, the ability to cycle to work will be of great value to **Emergency Planning**, as it helps keep vital services and businesses going. In order to do so though, people need to possess bikes, be fit enough to ride them and have done enough **Practical Skills** to undertake roadside repairs.

Change is a complex process, involving many interlocking factors. The Resilience Wheel concept is designed to express this. Each section of the Wheel represents an important element of a joined up Resilience Plan. Moving forward into greater resilience depends upon a certain level of progress in all of these elements. In turn any progress, however small or isolated it seems, in any section feeds into resilience as a whole.

The Resilience Wheel, like any other wheel, has many uses.

You can examine an idea to see how it interacts with each section of the Wheel, as in the willow basket example. You can identify strategies to deal with barriers to greater resilience, as in cycling to work. You can use the chapters as a quick reference if you need a briefing on that subject for research or in a debate.

And you can design Resilience Plans.

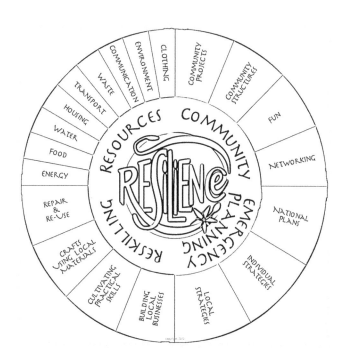

Chapter Three

Resilience Plans

The essence of a Resilience Plan is that everything you need to survive and thrive links together. Specialising in one direction needs to be balanced by competence in all the others, at both individual and community levels.

Think of some small actions you could take now. Buy organic potatoes, recycle from the whole house, grow some herbs, go to a community event, learn to crochet, pack a grab bag for emergencies. All these contribute to greater resilience for yourself and your community.

How can you encourage yourself to keep these up, to build on them, to involve other people?

Using the Resilience Wheel concept, you can design your personal or community plan. Consider where you are now in each section of the Wheel. I'll describe these in detail later on. Let's use **Food** from the **Resources** quadrant as an example.

Ideally, you would be sourcing many of your basic foods from local suppliers either directly or through shops, deliveries and markets. You'd know most of the people involved in the food chain personally. You'd grow a lot of fresh produce yourself, or harvest it from your community garden.

Not many people in Britain will be able to tick all these boxes, so we'll look at the other end of the scale.

You buy all your food from a large supermarket, eating mainly processed meals. You can't cook and don't know anyone who can show you how. If you have a garden at all, your landlord won't let you grow vegetables. In an emergency, you would depend on food aid being brought to you rather than being able to support yourself on surrounding resources for a while.

Imagine a scale from one to ten, with the highest score being for the ideal situation. Where do you think you are on this scale? What actions could you take to improve your score, and what barriers might you need to deal with?

Learning to cook basic meals with ingredients is an easy place to start. If you can't get on with cookery books or on-line instructions, try looking for a local group who may be of assistance.

Set yourself targets. Cook one more meal every week until packaged food is an occasional indulgence. Be realistic - you may need to manage your time differently – but be persistent. Remember every little action helps.

Now, how can you support local food production? The first step is to use your consumer power and buy it.

Where's your nearest shop? Can you get fresh meat and vegetables there? If not, this may need the help of the **Community** quadrant. If you join together in bulk orders, the shop may be able to bring in these items. Meanwhile find the nearest place which sells locally sourced food, even if you have to drive there.

Gradually reduce your dependence on supermarkets by supporting independent outlets. Thus food supplies become sourced locally and distributed around a larger area, rather than being shipped in and concentrated in one place. The need for transport is reduced, meaning less consumption of fuel and a more resilient system.

Grow herbs on your balcony, turn one of your flower beds into a vegetable patch, dig up some of the lawn, learn about gardening. Can you get an allotment? Even a small patch of fresh greens will provide essential vitamins to supplement tinned and dried food stores in an emergency.

How to create a Resilience Plan for yourself

Read the rest of the book. Identify some small actions in each section whereby you could increase your level of personal, practical resilience.

As an individual, you can direct your energy towards

- learning to use energy and resources responsibly
- respecting traditional crafts and spending money with local businesses
- seeking ways of strengthening your local community
- informing yourself about preparation for emergencies

As part of a community, you could
- work together to acquire and conserve resources
- develop the use of local resources and form buying groups to support craftspeople
- engage in community resilience projects and network with other groups
- form an emergency plan in liaison with the relevant authorities

Where are you now? You'll find more details about your personal resilience assessment in Appendix One. Once you have identified your present level, you can build on it. What can you do next?

Appendix Two outlines ways in which you can work to increase your practical resilience in a steady and measurable fashion. The essence of resilience is adaptability. Testing out various strategies may highlight issues that weren't considered, or couldn't be predicted.

Keeping a record will help. It's useful to colour in the sections of the Resilience Wheel as you feel you are making progress in them. This allows you to see areas you haven't dealt with, where you need to apply conscious effort. These will not be your favourite things. **Emergency Planning** tends to be the quadrant most people neglect. There are suggestions about ways of engaging with this later.

The interaction of the essential elements of practical resilience needs to be considered. At some point in every section, you'll be unable to increase your resilience level until other sections have caught up. Sometimes this is just a question of waiting for public awareness to become effective. Attend to your progress in the rest of the Wheel when this happens, staying alert for opportunities to overcome barriers.

This is a long term process, but at each stage your quality of life should improve. Conserving energy and resources reduces the cost of living. Informed consumer spending increases the prosperity of local businesses, who encourage the development of local resources. The existence of managed local resources is resilient, and on the way there a rather surprising amount of money is created to fund jobs in the area.

The task of achieving a truly sustainable and resilient global community seems daunting and personal efforts can feel dwarfed by the scale of change needed. Remember that we arrived at this place one choice at a time, and this is how we can move forward into a future with quality of life, natural harmony and hope.

Resilience is up to you.

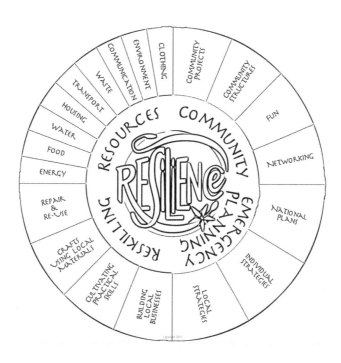

Chapter Four

Introduction to Resources

Energy and resources are inextricably linked. Resources such as coal, oil or food produce energy, which is then used to extract and process other resources. The materials you see around you - your furniture, clothing, cars and gadgets - are created using energy and will sooner or later interact with energy as they decay or are refashioned into other resources.

The availability of energy is a key factor in the nature of the resources you are able to draw on in everyday life. In this sense, energy is the underlying resource.

Energy is required to grow food, whether as manual labour or as diesel for tractors. We need energy to drive pumps and filtration plants for our supply and disposal of water. Products are brought to us and collected for recycling using energy. Processing cloth, maintaining communication systems and building homes all require energy.

Where does this come from?

Human labour was the first source of energy. People collected food, gathered and processed fibres or skins for clothing, built homes by hand. Working together and sharing skills enabled them to improve their standard of living – and their resilience. A well fed population with the leisure to be creative has a better chance of surviving adverse conditions.

With the advent of agriculture and settled life, domestic animals began to contribute to the energy available. Heavy pulling, carrying or lifting could be achieved by a single horse instead of a number of people, who were then able to go off and do other things. The energy input was significant; one man takes over three months to till a single hectare, a task which a horse could accomplish in a week.

Preparing grain for bread making has always been a time consuming part of the 'daily grind'. The harnessing of wind and water energy in mills which produced the community's flour saved yet more manual labour. Other simple machines were powered by treadmills, the energy supplied by animals.

Fire was used to supply domestic heat and light, in forging metals and firing pots. People were aware of the power of steam, but rarely used it save in novelty devices or to impress credulous worshippers with moving idols.

Developments in mining techniques and metal working increased the need for coal – used in extracting iron from ore. Keeping up with the demand for coal presented problems such as mine flooding which had to be solved by inventing more machinery. The Newcomen engine, invented in 1712, used the energy of steam generated by a coal fired boiler to pump water out of mines in order to get more coal.

Now plentiful supplies of iron and coal were to hand, steam engine designs proliferated and the Industrial Revolution took off in earnest. No longer did forests need to be felled to fuel the machines. Instead, they took their energy from deep beneath the earth where it lay in seemingly inexhaustible supply. Each pound of coal contained the same energy as ten days' work by a person.

With the clouds of noxious smoke billowing over the land and the forced relocation of entire communities from rural areas to labour in the new factory towns, it is difficult to see how this was a great improvement for many people. However, the new steam driven transport system could carry loads and travel at speeds never before possible, with major implications for the distribution of food and other goods.

Petroleum began to look interesting when it was distilled into kerosene for lamp oil, replacing expensive whale oil. Other products were soon on the market and the demand for crude oil encouraged supply. Oil began to overtake coal as the main fuel consumed by industrialised societies in the 1950s.

Natural gas sometimes occurs alone but is usually a byproduct of oil extraction. Although cleaner than coal gas, transporting it to customers required the development of fairly advanced technology and it used to be burned off. Now natural gas is piped from source and has largely replaced coal in domestic heating.

In 2012, the average person in Britain used around ten barrels of oil every year. Four barrels contain as much energy as a human being can produce in a lifetime of manual labour. Our current lifestyle, from cradle to grave and in the absence of fossil fuels, would need the support of over two hundred people each.

This is clearly ludicrous, as these people would need the work of many other people to feed and clothe them until most of the population was living at a subsistence level in order to support a tiny handful able to live as we do now. Without the oil-fuelled infrastructure of a military-industrial complex however, it would be difficult to keep up the necessary level of oppression.

Fossil fuels were created a long time ago, involving processes which took millions of years. They cannot be replaced once used up, and the evidence is that easily accessible sources are limited while global demand is increasing. If Britain retains its current 2% share of the world energy market – by no means certain as producers become reluctant to sell their remaining supplies – its people will soon have to get by on a mere six barrels per year each.

This seems a drastic reduction, yet it is no cause to expect to be shivering in the dark. Transport accounts for over a quarter of our energy use; a shift to more local economies can make significant savings. Renewables are independent of the supply of oil and can be developed to fill this energy gap. Creating energy closer to where it is used rather than feeding it into a centralised grid would cut down on power wasted in transmission.

The **Resources** quadrant of the Resilience Wheel lists nine key essentials. You can manage the energy use in each of these within your current lifestyle. Each is integrated into a resilient whole, so that no effort is wasted.

Growing even the tiniest amount of food reduces the overall energy required for transport. The herbs on your balcony inspire a neighbour to cultivate an allotment. Selling you the surplus seasonal vegetables encourages them to form a growing association. Soon there is a market stall, a shop. Meat is bought in from nearby farms through community supported agriculture. More money remains in the area and jobs are created.

Reusing, repairing and recycling reduce the amount of energy needed for industry and move the circulation of money to smaller firms and individual craftspeople. More community living, learning to share resources and building resilient off-grid housing estates are all strategies which can help reduce overall energy requirements.

While we still have access to the tremendous energy contained in fossil fuels, we should use it to clean up our land and develop skills old and new, enabling us to live without having to devote ourselves to mere survival in a depleted and toxic environment.

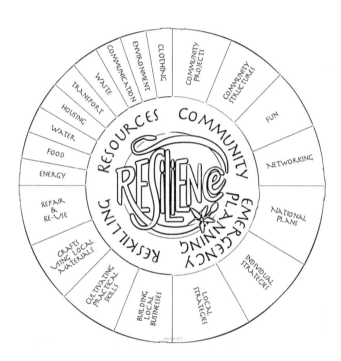

Chapter Five

Energy

Energy use affects every aspect of your life. When considering resilience in resources, you must always consider energy cost.

This section covers some of the energy you use directly, the way your home is heated, how you cook, the power you use for lighting and running appliances. In this country, we are conditioned to think of electricity as something that just comes out of the wall in an infinite stream, the only constraints on its use being the price.

Then there is a problem with the power distribution network and suddenly electricity is not there at all! This lacks resilience.

Within a resilient household, we are looking at using a limited amount of electricity to best effect. The ultimate goal is to provide your essential needs from a locally generated supply. To achieve full 'off-grid' status, you will need to reduce your consumption, explore the use of storage batteries and work with your community to share power.

Price and cost are not the same. It is just as important to invest effort in lifestyle changes as to spend money on renewables. Simple actions taken now can begin your move towards energy security.

Much of our electricity comes from power stations. Producing each unit of this easily transportable power takes about two and a half units of energy from sources such as coal, oil or gas. We can use these sources directly in our homes as well, for heating and cooking. Most homes use a combination of electricity and gas for their energy needs.

On average in the UK, almost 60% of domestic energy use is taken up in heating. Hot water accounts for another 25% with cooking, lighting and appliances using 16%. Reducing your personal energy use is resilient and saves money.

Heating is clearly a good place to look for results. The recent drive to improve the energy efficiency of houses has been very successful. New building regulations insist on many features in new houses which reduce heat wastage by a significant amount, while there are various grant programmes available to insulate older properties. Heating systems are more efficient, modern lighting uses less energy due to low energy bulbs and LEDs (Light Emitting Diodes).

Although energy use in the UK was the highest it had ever been at the turn of the century, domestic gas and electricity consumption fell by 24.7% between 2005 and 2011, according to the Office of National Statistics. These energy saving measures make it possible to respond to an increase in price by cutting use. How can you do this?

Could your home insulation be improved to keep heat in for longer? Your house loses about 35% of its heat through the walls, 25% by way of the roof or ceiling and 10% through double glazed windows. Only 15% is lost through the floor because heat rises, and draughts account for another 15% loss.

There are small, low cost actions you can take now. Have double curtains for the winter, make draught excluders for the doors. Check that your hot water tank and loft are insulated.

Learn your heating system. It should have a timer. Can you turn it off if you are out during the day? It will probably be controlled by a thermostat as well; find it. The recommended setting of 21*C may be too high if all the household are healthy. Lower temperatures save money and can discourage mould growth. Bring it down over a few weeks to 17*C.

Wear soft jumpers and fluffy socks around the house, cuddle a hot water bottle in the evenings. Winter is cold, get used to it; work with the seasons. If you're alone in the house, supplement a low ambient temperature with a 500 watt oil filled radiator beside you.

Electricity is a dry heat, while burning gas creates water. In a properly installed gas boiler, this should be vented outside as steam. A free standing gas fire, though, releases one litre of water into a room for every litre of gas used. Open the windows on sunny winter days to circulate fresh air.

Issues with damp in your home are closely related to heating. To help with these, and with planning major activities such as wall insulation or double glazing there are free advice centres.

Find them on the Internet, or through your local council.

Reduce other energy use in your home too. Turn lights off if you leave a room for more than five minutes. It isn't true that they take more energy to turn on and off. Replace current bulbs with LED varieties where possible. These do not contain mercury vapour.

Buy rechargeable AA and AAA batteries for toys and gadgets. It's good to have a box where your family can leave used ones for recharging, as they are expensive to lose. They each last several years though, soon repaying the initial investment. They require little power to charge, so can be kept going on your emergency system.

Pay attention to the power consumption information, the 'green ratings', when you buy a new household appliance. Do you need it at all? Vacuum cleaners and washing machines are essential – they destroy the eggs of fleas and other parasites. A dishwasher or tumble drier may be less important. Could you hire or share a carpet cleaner, lawn mower or hedge trimmer?

There are a number of websites and organisations who can advise you here. You should be able to understand your energy bills, and know where most of it is being used. Devices can be bought or borrowed to record consumption for individual items. Be aware of the standby costs for various gadgets and turn them off when not in use.

Every saving in energy is a saving in money as well as a move towards a more sustainable way of life.

Renewable energy

Coal, oil and gas are all finite resources. Even if there are hundreds of years worth left to exploit, they will run out eventually. The other problem with fossil fuels is that they are only found in certain areas. Their use depends on a complex distribution system which supports centralisation rather than localism.

The only energy resources available to most individuals and communities for development are renewables.

The main argument against these seems to be that they would never produce 'enough'. Enough for what? Enough to leave all the lights blazing and appliances on standby in every home? Enough to heat your house to the point where you can wander around in a T shirt all winter?

They probably won't.

However, if you are looking at a basic system which can act as an emergency back up with normal peak demand handled by a national grid, then there could very well be enough.

We have the technology to equip every community with their own energy supply – a windmill, solar panels, hydroelectric mills using the old millstreams. These could be owned and operated by the community, who would need to make real and immediate decisions, thus reviving social cohesion.

As members of the community, you would be able to vote on your own electricity prices. You could agree to use high energy devices such as washing machines only at certain times of day to avoid having to cope with peak demand, which would need to be bought in. Automatic timers could make this easy.

The more ambitious could follow the example of the German town of Wildpoldsried.....

"In 1997, people of Wildpoldsried, in some cases acting as individuals, began a series of projects that produce renewable energy. The first efforts were wind turbines and biomass digesters for cogeneration of heat and power. In the time since, new work has included a number of energy conservation projects, more wind and biomass use, small hydro plants, photovoltaic panels on private houses, and district heating. Tied to this are ecological flood control and wastewater systems.
Today, the effects of this are an unforeseen level of prosperity resulting in construction of nine new community buildings, including a school, gymnasium, and community hall, complete with solar panels. There are three companies operating four biogas digesters with a fifth under construction. There are seven windmills with two more on the way. One hundred and ninety private households are equipped with solar, which pays them dividends. The district heating network has 42 connections. There are three small hydro power plants.
By 2011, Wildpoldsried produced 321% more energy than it needs and generated 4.0 million Euro

in annual revenue. At the same time, there was a 65% reduction in the town's carbon footprint. Three years later, the village was producing five times the energy it consumed." (Quote from Wikipedia)

Could you participate in a community windmill, biomass or hydroelectric plan? Surplus energy can be sold to finance maintenance and to pay back investors. A serious attempt to put such ideas into action, bringing decent resources to bear and involving the skills and creativity of real communities, is a far better use of our resources than arguing over which type of mega power plant to build.

Energy Resilience Plan

Here are ten steps you can take. The first ones deal with the current situation for most people – living in a house which has not been designed with resilience in mind, and without the resources to make immediate major changes. The last five describe the efforts you could take towards informed use of locally generated power.

The materials in Appendix One allow you to express your practical energy resilience as a percentage score. You can then work on improving it in an organised and targeted fashion.

- Understand your energy bills. Know how they relate to your heating and hot water. Look at the green credentials of your supplier. Do you support their company policy?
- Insulate.
- Turn off lights and don't leave devices on standby.
- Use rechargeable batteries for small gadgets.
- Understand candle safety in case you have to use them in an emergency. Have proper holders so they don't fall over. These should be made of metal or ceramics. Stand night-lights and pillar candles on saucers to protect the surface beneath from heat and wax. Never put a candle underneath a shelf, nor anywhere near curtains, hangings and piles of loose paper.
- Plan to replace appliances as they wear out with lower energy options, including lifestyle changes.
- Learn about 12 volt systems, battery storage and small scale domestic renewables, such as portable solar PV panels. Shops catering for caravans and motor homes are good places

to look for this equipment. Find out how to use regulators and inverters. Could you set up an improvised off-grid system capable of running a few lights and keeping a radio working? How would you address safety issues here?

- Calculate how much of your home could run on a supply of 2 kilowatts (2000 watts). How much more energy would you need? Does it all have to be electrical?

At this point, your drive to resilience may encounter a barrier. Not everyone is in a position to build themselves a new house or join an off-grid community. Resilience as a whole may need to move forward to allow you these options.

You can still prepare for them by research and learning, increasing your awareness of energy use. If you are clear about what you need, you will be better placed to identify opportunities and make the most of them.

- Imagine how your home could be designed to allow you to use more renewable energy. Look for these features if you are moving. What sort of **Housing** is available? What **Transport** would connect you to your work?
- Research **Community** power schemes - there are a number of successful ones. Learn about larger scale renewables. What is your **Environment** rich in – wind, sun, running water, tides?

Chapter Six

Food

For most people in this country, their major source of food is the supermarket. This is neither sustainable nor resilient.

The popularity of, and gradual dependence on, supermarkets grew with personal car ownership. There used to be large covered markets in town centres, easily accessible by public transport, but not well furnished with car parking. Fed up with carrying heavy bags of shopping home in the rain, people were naturally drawn to shopping by car. Soon out of town supermarkets, taking advantage of cheaper land to install large car parks, grew to service this desire.

Much of the money spent there leaves the local economy. High Street shops run by family firms wither and die from lack of custom. Farmers go bankrupt in the midst of thousands of potential customers for their produce.

Here, more than anywhere else, you can make a difference. Change the way you buy your food, cook from ingredients, grow your own. Inform yourself and use your consumer power.

Find your nearest farm shop. They often give a better deal on quality meat than supermarkets – if not, ask them what you could do to help them bring prices down, such as initiate a buyers' group. Buy in bulk and freeze a month's supply if your busy lifestyle doesn't allow regular trips – or maybe they will deliver.

Look for sources of fresh local fruit and vegetables – preferably organic as the use of agricultural chemicals is not sustainable practise, nor is it resilient. There are a number of box schemes which can deliver a regular supply of produce to you.

Locally grown and milled flour is enjoying a revival; lay in supplies and begin to bake your own bread. You can blend different sorts of grain and create your personal favourite loaf! Many varieties are available; some with reduced gluten. Freezing is the best storage method for breads containing no preservatives, whereas refrigeration enhances staling. Pre-slice a loaf and toast the slices direct from frozen.

Adapt your cooking habits to reflect what you have available, plan meals ahead. Go shopping with a list and stick to it. Don't go into a supermarket when you are hungry!

Even if you have no outdoor growing space at all, you can still cultivate herbs by the window or sprout seeds. The smallest balcony or patio can house a few pots of rocket, cress or mustard for fresh salad leaves.

If you have a garden, dig up the lawn and grow food. There are unused gardens which could be cultivated and the produce shared. Begin by identifying the type of soil:

- Clay is muddy in winter and hard in summer. Weeds will break if pulled rather than come up with roots
- Sandy soil is powdery in summer and might have a layer of actual sand if you dig down
- Loam is the best; it is dark and rich looking. Weeds can be pulled up whole

A kit from the garden shop will tell you if the soil is acid or alkali, and what to do about it.

Dig over new ground to prepare it, or cover it with sheets of card to suppress weeds and plant through this. As you work, observe the way the sun falls on your growing space at different times of day.

Plants growing in shade, even small localised areas, will be slower but better able to stand periods of very hot sun. Put delicate crops, which have to be started in a greenhouse and only put out once all danger of frost is past, in the sunniest places. You can buy these from other growers.

A weed is best defined as a plant growing where you want something different to thrive. Having a wild patch is useful to encourage helpful insects and animals. An area with a lot of shade is good for this. You should dig up the fat white roots of bindweed and throw them away. Dandelions and dock will also sprout from root fragments, but at least these are edible.

If you have an outside tap available, this is a bonus. Otherwise, before you start, fill a bucket with water to rinse the worst of the mud from your hands before going back inside, or handling seeds and fragile seedlings. If you are gardening some distance from the nearest water, carry a couple of two litre water bottles in your bucket. Finding a way to capture and store rain water should be one of your priorities here.

You will only need a spade or fork for the initial work, so you could borrow rather than buy at first. A rake is good to level out the prepared soil. A trowel and hand fork are the best tools once you have started, and a hoe is useful to weed a large space.

Don't tread on the soil if you can possibly avoid it, as this will compact it and make life harder for your plants. Place paths at intervals, made of bricks, large stones, planks of wood or carpet strips, so that you can reach your plants without stepping on the soil. If you are making raised beds to deal with wet or poisoned soil, build them quite narrow with paths between.

Plant native nut and fruit trees such as hawthorn, blackthorn, hazel and rosehip for a hedge instead of privet. Food trees take years to mature, so start now. For colour, grow edible blossoms such as nasturtium, or a selection of bee-friendly flowers.

Allotments in both town and country are becoming more popular and can be a major source of basics such as potatoes and onions. Careful management can keep your family in seasonal vegetables all year, with a surplus to trade. Private landowners may be prepared to rent out land for growing.

Remember that organically grown food properly prepared contains more natural vitamins and minerals than factory farmed and processed foods. You can change to healthier eating habits through paying more attention to where your food comes from.

Store a collection of the tinned and dried food which your family or community use regularly. Keep this supply rotating and take reasonable advantage of special offers to restock. With fresh vegetables from your own growing space, you could dine well for quite some time in the event of a major disruption of services.

Once you begin to eat your own produce, you will notice that there are a lot of peelings and leafy parts left over. Use these to make compost; there are instructions on-line for using both heaps and bins. Cardboard and newspaper are good for extra fibre, but glossy magazines often contain too much toxic ink. You can turn waste into soil indoors using a Bokashi bucket, or dig a trench outside and bury it raw. Peas and beans thrive on this.

There is much debate about the role of meat in future diets. Animals need food crops, some of which could be used by people instead. However, if you were self-sufficient in vegetables and fruit, the waste generated in preparing these for the table would feed a number of animals. The concept of 'default meat' attempts to quantify the amount of produce you could obtain just as a side effect of small holding. For more information on this, refer to the book 'Meat – a benign extravagance' by Simon Fairlie.

Current estimates of default meat in this country are around half a kilogram of meat per person per week. This doesn't sound so bad until you realise that dairy products are part of it. Five litres of milk are the equivalent of a kilo of meat. One litre of milk makes about 150 grams of cheese and only an ounce of butter. This explains the popularity of lard as a cooking fat in the old days!

You could, of course, decide to use more land to raise animals. Keep in mind that this would give you less food value than growing crops for yourself. Cultivating oil seeds such as hemp provides nutritious feed cake as well as cooking oil. Resilient communities of the future will need to consider issues like these.

Having brought resilience into your own kitchen, look at the ways in which a community can work together to source good quality food and support their local producers. Forming a community food co-op is one. Perhaps you could work with a local shop for storage and distribution. Or you could look at community supported agriculture (CSA), which is a partnership between farmers and the local community, providing mutual benefits and reconnecting people to the land where their food is grown.

Small food producers face a difficult time in competition with supermarkets. To boost our local economies and provide jobs, we need to help them add value to their products by processing it. Cheese, butter and yogurt sold at retail prices are far more profitable than milk if the customers are there.

The catering business is an important factor in the British food network; support the independent pubs, restaurants and cafes in your area. Institutions and corporations have large staff catering budgets – lobby them to source locally too.

Resilience in your food supply network is dependent on as much as possible being grown in this country. The use of chemicals to increase yields has proved to have many drawbacks apart from harmful effects on human health – water pollution, expense, damage to wildlife, loss of vitamins and minerals in food. Large fields growing a single crop managed by machine may not be the most economic way of maximising production after all.

At the very least, you have to be prepared to accept muddy or oddly-shaped vegetables, unusual types of edible fish, seasonal shortages and other minor inconveniences to support the economics of a move to food resilience.

Food Resilience Plan

Here are ten steps you can take. There's been a good deal of activity around food growing so you may already be involved with organisations such as the Master Gardener project or the Incredible Edible towns who grow vegetables in hanging baskets and public flowerbeds.

It's not that long since nearly everyone grew a lot of their own food, without expensive chemicals. We can still access that old fashioned know-how if people start taking an interest in gardening again.

- Cook from ingredients at least twice a week. Try out new recipes.
- Cut down on food waste by shopping with a list. Plan ahead to use up leftovers.
- Grow herbs and salad leaves where ever you can – grow more adventurous vegetables if you have a garden.
- Buy Local! Shop in your High Street or have fresh produce delivered from your nearest farm shop.
- Learn which foods contain important vitamins and minerals and work out a balanced diet.
- Maintain a store of tinned and dried foods for emergencies.
- Is there a food co-op in your area? A neighbourhood buying group or community supported agriculture association? Could you start one?
- Find your nearest available growing space – your garden, an allotment, a field or verge – and make a plan for cultivating it, including a strategy for sourcing any help or permissions needed.

- Go on a guided foraging walk to identify edible wild plants.
- Try living on your 'default' meat and dairy for a week. What other foods might you need more of?

Growing even a little food, and keeping some emergency stores, helps you manage your shopping trips to make the most of bargains and to support local businesses. Cooking from fresh ingredients is cheaper than buying processed food, and more nutritious. People often overeat because their diet is unbalanced.

For more details on growing and preparing food, see 'Recipes for Resilience - Common Sense Cooking for the 21st Century' by Elizabeth J Walker.

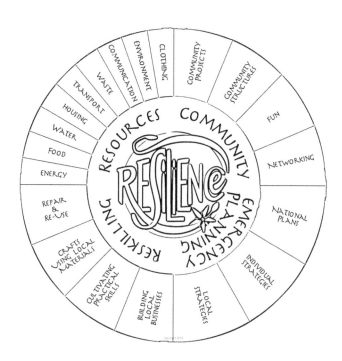

Chapter Seven

Water

The influence of water is written clearly on our landscape, from glacier-rounded hills to coastlines carved by the sea. Water is essential to every aspect of our lives, and there is a great deal to be learned about it.

A daily minimum of two litres of water is necessary for survival, and in some countries obtaining even this small amount can be a challenge. In water-rich Britain, an ordinary household using accessible water conservation measures will use around eighty litres daily per person. A third of this is used as toilet flush, another quarter in the bathroom, the rest in the kitchen and garden. All this water is clean enough to drink.

Unless you have your own well or spring, supplying this water to your taps requires energy and a complex infrastructure to clarify, filter and disinfect it before delivery. This begins at a raw water collection point, such as a reservoir. It is transferred to purification plants through huge underground tunnels.

From there, it is delivered to the consumer. The pH value of the water is controlled to protect the pipework. Old iron pipes can colour it red, and the corrosion of copper gives it a metallic taste. Early systems used lead, which is a soft metal and easily shaped into plumbing, but this was highly toxic.

Energy is added to the system to create water pressure which drives the flow. Using the natural flow of gravity is best, but sometimes pumps have to be included. The water supply in blocks of flats is almost always dependent on having mains electricity or generator fuel. It would be more resilient to use solar power from panels on the roof.

Improving home insulation in modern houses has saved energy. The next design issue which needs to be addressed is water use. In order to reuse grey water from the bath or shower (not kitchen waste or toilet flush) efficiently, the plumbing system of a house must be redesigned. This is best done before building as retrofitting is awkward.

Working around existing structures is harder, but still possible; there are many ways to conserve water. Reduce the water in old style toilet cisterns using plastic packs. Get a bath siphon to reuse this water in the garden or to flush the toilet. Use a water saving setting on washing machines and flow restrictors on shower heads.

Fix leaks promptly. A dripping tap can waste 15 litres of water a day. Be aware which of your pipes are exposed to cold, and what to do if your plumbing freezes. You need to know where your internal stop tap is and how to turn it off, in case of burst pipes or other problems. A tight fitting bath plug is a good investment. In an emergency, you can store clean water there.

Water is also used to carry away waste. Once used, it flows – or is pumped – away from the household to a sewage treatment plant. Energy is needed to purify the water before releasing it into the wild.

Solid waste was once important in the tanning industry and in making saltpetre for gunpowder. With the advent of sewage systems, it was often piped out to fertilise large grasslands outside the cities. These sewage farms were discontinued when the water became too contaminated with pollutants.

If you are designing an 'eco-village', you may be considering a reed bed system to deal with waste water. These use living plants and many chemicals which you casually wash down the sink damage them. As with all off-grid solutions, a lifestyle change is required.

Experiment with eco-products. Try making your own household cleaning materials using less toxic ingredients such as lemon juice, vinegar and bicarbonate of soda. Be warned - a dash of bleach is not going to improve your vinegar-based disinfectant!

Never mix bleach, or other products containing chlorine, with anything but pure water. Read the ingredients. If you're not sure what a chemical is, look it up on-line. Mixing chlorine with acids, like vinegar, or with ammonia, such as found in many other commercial cleaning agents, causes the immediate release of very poisonous gases.

Don't mix hydrogen peroxide with other substances either. Be careful when cleaning drains as well. If one product hasn't unblocked them, call a plumber rather than trying a different chemical which may not get on very well with the first one.

Follow the advice given about safe disposal when you throw away your shed-full of poisonous garden chemicals and resolve to garden organically from now on.

Learn which manufactured products cause the most pollution and try to find alternatives. If you buy those made locally, you will be aware of any damage to the water system they may cause.

The relationship of water with industry and agriculture has always been difficult. Despite the success of modern legislation in cleaning up a good number of watercourses, the amount of agrochemicals used each year is still a problem.

Nitrates and phosphates stimulate plant growth and, when added as fertiliser, produce good crop yield. These chemicals are washed into the water system from farmland and gardens. They feed blooms of algae which deplete the water of oxygen as they decay, so killing all the fish and seafood. This process is called eutrophication.

Encouraging small scale farming, where different high yield techniques are employed, requires more consumer interest and better support from various authorities. The costs of industrial agriculture need to be joined up.

The use of chemical fertilisers could be balanced by a network of small and relatively undisturbed streams. These can remove most of these nitrates before they concentrate. The existing natural network has been diverted and consolidated into larger waterways over the years. Bigger fields suitable for machinery use and for raising cattle were created. Crops such as willow, which survive being waterlogged, have been marginalised. The productive capacity of marsh land has been ignored.

Rainwater moves much faster through this new streamlined drainage system, resulting in flooding. The contents of sewage systems mix with the floodwater, leaving a residue of toxic silt behind. A single cubic metre of water weighs a tonne; its relentless power causes widespread damage.

This power can be harnessed in more controlled circumstances. Flowing rivers have driven mills since ancient times, mainly for grinding flour. Some were used to power industrial processes, as in early cotton factories, but steam engines soon took over.

Fundamentally, electricity is created by spinning a magnet and a coil of wire in relation to each other. The physical motion of the water can be transmitted to a generating device. From there, the electricity provided is used locally or fed into a larger grid. Reviving water mills can play a significant role in rebuilding resilience. They can generate electricity or drive machinery directly. Microhydro systems, creating under 100 kilowatts, are common in developing countries.

The first person to combine the newly invented electrical generator with hydropower was William Armstrong, who used it to run a light for his art gallery in 1878. More hydroelectric schemes were swiftly developed. By 1920 they were responsible for nearly half the power produced in the USA. Today, across the world, they provide over 16% of the total electricity used.

The schemes continued to get larger, dependent on dams rather than natural rivers. Interactions with flood control, navigation and the surrounding ecology became more significant. Millions of people have been displaced from the land used by huge reservoirs. The volume of water held back in these causes catastrophic flooding if the dam fails.

Despite these drawbacks, large scale hydroelectric plants are so cost effective that they are referred to as 'white coal'. Once built, they last for decades and require little management.

The power of the tide, driven by gravitational forces, can also be exploited. Tide powered mills dating back to the 6th century have been discovered in Ireland. The incoming tides filled lagoons, from which water flowed out in a controlled manner to drive mill wheels. Today, this water displacement spins turbines for electricity production.

Tides are a predictable energy source, but tidal power has been slow to develop. Construction costs are high, and there were not many suitable sites available. New developments in design and in turbine technology are opening up some of the marginal sites, encouraged by the financial successes of early projects.

Wave power differs from tidal and ocean current energy. It's really a form of wind power. The water itself does not move. Far out to sea, low pressure zones cause ripples. These are fanned by the wind, catching its energy like a sail. The ripples become waves and eventually break on the shore, often having travelled thousands of miles. The rise and fall of these waves contains the collected wind energy and this can be harvested by the use of moving elements.

Wave energy may be most useful around harbours and in coastal defences. As the aim of wave power is to capture as much energy as possible from the flux, the waves beyond the device are smaller, less destructive. Heavy duty concrete structures can be used in coastal installations.

The potential energy generated by the sea is significant; enough to supply thousands of houses. A reasonably sized wave converter or tidal engine established on the shoreline could power a desalination plant, a fish cannery or harbour facilities.

Water as a transport system in this country used to be far more important. In prehistoric times the dense forests on land often made it easier to travel along the coast or up rivers by boat. At the start of the Industrial Revolution the canal network was exploited for its ability to carry large loads.

Water transport is slow, and was soon replaced by rail. Today it is mainly used for leisure purposes, but could be integrated into a sustainable transport model for a lower energy, more relaxed future.

Water Resilience Plan

- Understand your water bills. They are usually calculated using cubic metres which are 1000 litres each. Pay attention to the dates detailing the period of use if you want to work out daily consumption per person.
- Use all available measures to conserve water in your house.
- Collect rainwater and reuse grey water where possible.
- Use handmade soaps to wash your hair rather than commercial shampoos. You will save on plastic bottles too. Handmade soaps use cold-processing methods, which are better for this purpose than factory-made soaps.
- Find, make and use cleaning products which cause minimum pollution.
- Keep your plumbing system in good repair, with exposed pipes insulated. Know where the water shut off tap is. Buy a bath plug that fits properly.
- Go and visit a reed bed system, a hydroelectric power station, a water treatment works.
- Learn how to make distilled water for drinking; study the use of ad hoc filtration systems for emergencies.
- Explore the inland waterways on a holiday or day out.
- Know the location of your nearest well or spring.

Chapter Eight

Housing

Modern houses have come a long way from traditional stone cottages and terraces heated by open fires, drawing water from a well nearby and growing basic foodstuffs in gardens or allotments.

Resilience has not been a priority in mainstream house design but there are a number of alternatives being developed. The concept of 'off grid' is important, which means being entirely independent of mains services. Off grid living is sustainable and cheap, but does involve more work from the householder. Electricity becomes a finite resource and this requires a lifestyle change.

There are a number of features which could be built in to new houses to maintain essential services if normal supplies are cut off in an emergency. Sometimes it can take weeks for them to be fully restored.

Good insulation means that a minimum of heat, like that from a 'flowerpot stove', can keep the chill off. There may be some grants available for retrofitting. Insulating solid walls and installing double glazing will make a big difference.

Most double glazing frames are made of PVC, a form of plastic; oil based and difficult to dispose of. They are prone to crack and are resistant to repair. Sustainably sourced hardwood is ideal. Avoid metal frames as they will conduct heat out of the building.

The choice of insulation materials is important too. Those made from fossil fuels, such as polystyrene, are non-breathable and may contribute to damp problems. Use natural materials, such as wool, hemp products or even cork, if you can afford them. They will absorb the effects of temporary changes in humidity indoors.

Fibreglass is made out of molten glass. It contains a high percentage of recyclate, up to 30%, and this could be increased. Currently most varieties use toxic formaldehyde as a binder, but this is changing. Cellulose insulation, such as Warmcel, is made by shredding old newspapers and is a cheap option.

Few houses are built with an alternative to centralised supplies for heating and cooking in mind. Even solid fuel central heating may need careful attention if mains water is not available to replenish the header tank. The pump could be run on battery power through your inverter in the absence of other electricity. It will not be designed to do so, but the system may overheat if the water does not circulate.

Have a cooker which runs on bottled gas, or convert an existing one with a simple kit. The gas bottle will be kept outside, but a safety cage isn't needed for domestic use. A registered gas technician will be able to install this.

Never use a barbecue or other charcoal burning device to heat a room or to cook indoors; they give off dangerous amounts of carbon monoxide and could quickly kill you.

Water conservation and rainwater capture can help if water is in limited supply. You may need to collect it from a bowser or street tap if supplies are interrupted. 'Grey water' is that used in a bath, shower or washing machine and can be reused as toilet flush, to water a garden or wash a car.

Rainwater from your roof can be stored in plastic barrels. You may be able to use the gradients in your garden to fill other barrels in handy locations or to set up drip irrigation. These systems are especially useful in allotments and polytunnels.

Your home is where you prepare food and store your supplies. In the days before electric fridges, many had walk-in pantries. These were usually built on the north wall, and were surprisingly cool. Growing and preserving your own food requires space often lacking in modern kitchens. Many are designed for people prepared to accept a diet consisting of packaged meals heated in a microwave.

If you are moving house, look for storage space. A floored loft is the most useful for emergency tinned and dried supplies. Lofts are subject to extreme temperature variations, and summer heat needs to be taken into account for other stored foods.

Eco-friendly products can be found for a range of home improvements. Sourcing British timber is very difficult. None of the DIY chain stores sell it, and few sawmills; you have to find a specialist supplier. Encouraging these is important.

When planning a project, see how much of the material you can find second hand. Explore the fascinating reclamation yards, or check out boot sales. Every tool shed needs a good clear out from time to time. Is there a charity which can use your surplus stock?

Many household paints contain poisonous chemicals. These create a pollution problem. Read the labels; the environmental information is clearly displayed. Learn which types of paint are appropriate for each purpose, and recycle leftovers responsibly. Store unused paint correctly; if it freezes, it may spoil.

Houses are filled with furniture. Buy second hand where possible. Consider quality, ease of cleaning and comfort in purchases. Save money by prolonging the life of your existing furniture so that you can gradually replace it with the more expensive items made by local craftspeople.

There are courses, and information on the internet, for those prepared to create their own furniture. Scrap wood can be turned into many ingenious and practical items, polished up with your home made beeswax concoctions. Soft furnishings, such as rugs and curtains, are good for the novice to try. Upholstery is a more advanced skill, but very impressive.

Remember to look at the labels when choosing cleaning products, and avoid the most toxic. Some traditional methods, involving baking soda or vinegar, are still valid alternatives.

If you have a balcony or garden, put up a washing line. Make use of free solar power to dry your clothes. Barriers to this include rules set by the landlord and petty theft. You would have to work with the **Community** quadrant of the Resilience Wheel to overcome these.

Gardens are often overshadowed by tall panel fencing, made from imported conifer wood. Replace these with woven willow fence panels. These will let both light and wind through, providing privacy while not blowing down in every storm. A larger market for locally grown willow would encourage its use to mitigate flooding.

Meanwhile, growing vegetables requires sunlight. Find out which part of your garden gets most light and dig up a patch, or site large pots there. Sheds and other storage are best placed in the shaded areas. An advantage of community tool sharing is that only one really secure shed is needed for several people.

Gardening with your neighbours would often be easier if there was a different layout to modern housing estates. Privacy is encouraged at the expense of communication. There's not a lot of scope for major design changes once houses are built.

Some improvements on the standard estate plan can be made, such as the inclusion of large open spaces at frequent intervals for play areas and community gardens. A covered meeting place there could house a shop or a residents' co-operative. Using a temporary structure, such as a Portacabin, saves costs.

Car parking areas can be surfaced with grasscrete, allowing rain water to soak away rather than run off. This reduces the danger of flooding, both on the estate and downstream of it. Wildlife corridors should be established and sections of the estate linked with alleyways to help with social connection.

To add sustainable water and sewage facilities, however, really needs an integrated estate development, such as Eva-Lanxmeer in the Netherlands or Hockerton in Nottinghamshire. Each time a housing estate is built using current protocols, another opportunity is lost to create a resilient community.

The use of locally sourced materials in building is not encouraged, despite the huge trade deficit this generates for the UK. Planners approve large estates, which will be built using imports, yet refuse permission for individual straw bale houses.

Every year, British farmers generate enough straw as a byproduct of grain production to build over 600,000 homes. Cob is an even more local material. A cob house is built using the subsoil from its own foundations, mixed with a sandy aggregate and some straw. Both methods can provide comfortable houses with all modern conveniences. Prefabricated timber frame houses are also robust, cheap and can be designed to your own specifications.

The Passivhaus is an ultra low energy design, where controlling air flow and using insulation means that the building is heated solely by the people and appliances inside. The design, first piloted in 1988, is suitable for commercial premises as well as houses, and over 20,000 such buildings have been constructed. Photo-voltaics or windmills can supply electricity, making these independent of the grid for essential power.

If you are interested in getting involved with a fully resilient building project, they are still quite rare. Check the internet, or consider starting your own.

Housing Resilience Plan

- Insulate; learn about the types of materials available and which can be used in retrofitting.
- Use your outside space: put up a washing line, grow vegetables or herbs.
- Care for your furniture and look for locally made or second hand replacements.
- If you are planning a DIY project, try to source the materials so that your spending benefits your local economy. Consider the energy footprint and choose sustainable options.
- Know how to turn your mains services on and off, and how to make your house safe if you need to leave it in an evacuation.
- Consider how you could manage without a fridge or freezer. How would your shopping and eating habits need to change?
- Learn to make a table, a rocking chair, an upholstered settee.
- Know how to provide essential services in your house, both during an overnight interruption of mains supplies and one which lasts several weeks.
- Value garden and food storage space when looking for a different house. Consider its off-grid potential.
- Buy into a community eco-housing plan.

Chapter Nine

Transport

Begin by considering how you transport yourself, for this is the easiest thing for you to change.

Walking is the earliest form of transport and can still have a role in modern life. It is slow, you are not protected from the weather and cannot carry much, but it is cheap and keeps you fit. Ironically, it is in rural areas where everyday walking can be hardest, due to the distances separating people and facilities. If you live in a city, you may be able to walk to many places – work, shops, friends.

Try the Urban Walking Route Planner on-line where you can find a map between any two points, which includes your journey time, calorie burn, step count and carbon saving. It's quick, free, healthy and green!

Walking for pleasure is another way to keep fit while exploring your neighbourhood. Or take a bus further afield and a different bus home, so you are free from having to walk in a circle back to your car. Many people already enjoy walking holidays. The 'Walking Britain' website has maps, descriptions and pictures of walks all over the country, along with a useful beginners' guide and details of possible accommodation on the routes.

Then there is cycling, which has many of the same advantages as walking. You can carry more, but have to consider a safe place to leave your bike when you stop. Many workplaces are now providing facilities for staff who cycle in – showers, lockers to keep dry clothes, a secure bike store.

As with walking, cycling can be a leisure activity. You can get involved with the competitive sport aspect of it, or go on cycling holidays in Britain and abroad.

Sharing the roads with motor vehicles can be dangerous and there is a plan to extend a national cycle network across the country. This project is being promoted by Sustrans which was founded in Bristol in 1977 to help people travel in ways that benefit their health and the environment.

This cycle network is transforming everyday travel for millions of people countrywide. New bridges and crossings are being created to overcome busy roads, rivers and railways. These are linked to existing networks of walking and cycling routes, making it easier for people to use these for everyday journeys.

Technically, you can still travel on horseback in Britain, but this is fraught with difficulty and for the true pioneer! There are no hitching rails outside shops, and the etiquette of tethering your animals in a public place is long forgotten. Holidays involving horse riding are popular though, and riding schools can be found across the country. It's worth cultivating a basic competence in this skill, as it is very rewarding.

Having looked at the various low technology options, we now move on to motorised transport, whose development was made possible by the exploitation of fossil fuels, and the amount of energy they release. A litre of petrol has the energy value of over a week of human manual labour.

The personal car has been a huge success at an individual level. It allows you to travel protected from the weather, carrying almost anything you may need, going anywhere that the road network reaches with your entire family and the dog. People unable to walk or cycle due to disability are able to travel with far more ease.

Various factors have begun to make this less of an affordable luxury however. Fossil fuels are no longer as cheap and abundant as they were. The space required to accommodate all these cars is becoming a problem, from neighbourhood disputes about parking to gridlock in cities and the constant need to turn productive land into more roads. The exhaust gases poison the air and disposing of used cars has become an issue.

Depending upon being able to maintain a personal car under any circumstances is not resilient. Flood, snowfall or fuel shortages can bring your entire lifestyle to a halt.

The move away from always using a private car has a number of advantages though. Our communities have become distorted and fragmented by our increased mobility. Instead of being within walking distance, visiting friends and family often involves driving as they are so widely scattered. Getting to work, even to school, can be a long journey.

The alternatives need to be recreated and we need to start looking at how this can be done. Considering more sustainable methods of travel is a good start.

Public transport needs to be supported. Even if you have a car, you should consider making some journeys by other means, especially if you have to go into a large town where congestion is a problem. Plan ahead and book travel in advance for cheaper fares.

You could organise joint shopping trips with your neighbours, or share a taxi to see a show in town. Car sharing and community vehicle ownership are some other options that can be explored. City car clubs have vehicles parked all over major cities for their members' use; search for them on-line.

Flying is a controversial way to travel as it uses a lot of energy. Its main advantage is speed which allows you to access international destinations with plenty of time to enjoy a holiday or conduct important business. A more relaxed lifestyle and more use of the internet in business conferencing would reduce the importance of haste. Even so, there will always be some instances when a long journey has to be made quickly or when personal contact is necessary.

The Royal Aeronautical Society website is a useful resource when looking at the environmental impact of flying. It also considers issues around cargo flights, which brings us to the next function of transport – the movement of goods.

As an individual, it is challenging to influence freight traffic directly. It is a subject of global concern. You can support your local economy, thus reducing the amount of stuff that needs to be brought to you. Avoid buying food linked to high air miles – these are not just exotic produce but basics such as soya from America.

If you wish to pursue this topic further, you could research the amount of transport needed to bring you the things you see around you – don't forget the packaging! Identify a more sustainable option where you can and write to retailers encouraging them to use this. Get used to some foods being seasonal.

Forming a community group to share this information and exert more consumer power will be helpful.

Cargo vessels, rail and canal are more sustainable and resilient methods of carrying goods than are road or air transport. The adventurous among you could explore these options on a barge or cargo ship holiday. Dealing with the challenges involved in creating resilient freight transport will be assisted by progress made in other sections of the Resilience Wheel.

With **food** and **clothing** sourced from a local economy, there is less need for long distance haulage. Currently, recycled **waste** can be taken many miles from source, made into other things and then transported back to us. Drawing this process into the local economy cuts out the need for these return trips.

Inform yourselves and use your consumer power.

Transport Resilience Plan

The abundance of cheap fossil fuels has had a direct impact on transport. The way we move around has shaped our modern communities. The step from private car to shared transport will be a challenging one.

When shipping costs are so low that moving a sweat shirt half way around the world only costs a few cents, local manufacturers cannot compete with the low labour costs in the Far East. They need to be supported by people who can afford to pay the extra for goods made within our economy.

- Walk around your neighbourhood regularly.
- Use public transport at least once a month, even if you have a private car
- Choose to buy food and goods with the lowest transport costs in terms of energy used.
- Learn to ride and maintain a bicycle. Can you hire one nearby? Drive for fuel economy. You can keep your car serviced for efficiency, have the correct tyre pressures and reduce drag by removing roof racks when not in use.
- Make a transport plan for yourself in case of an emergency where you cannot use your own car.
- Work out how often you need the use of a large vehicle, or to go on long journeys. Could

you change to an electric or hybrid fuel car?

- Find out if there are there any car sharing schemes near you, either commercial or community run.
- Plan a holiday without flying. Make the travel part of the experience. Adventures will test your resilience.
- Design a community transport hub for your area. How might it work?

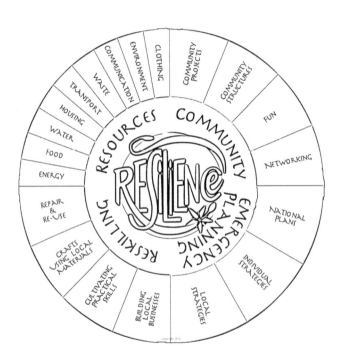

Chapter Ten

Waste

In the past few decades we have used up a third of the world's natural resources. Much of this has ended up in a huge and growing pile of rubbish at the end of the path from natural beauty through man made stuff to broken, used and discarded junk.

You can begin to tackle this problem at home, by looking at what you use and where it goes next.

How much do you waste?

Reducing consumption is the first step. A vast amount of the food bought in Britain is thrown away. Most of this could have been eaten. Plan your meals ahead of shopping and stick to a list. Keep an old fashioned kitchen notebook for ideas such as recipes for left overs.

Cooking from ingredients, rather than buying processed food, saves money. Dried food – flour, beans, barley – keeps well and is cheap. Improve your storage methods for perishable items.

Buying less, you'll be bringing home less packaging as well. There is far too much of this discarded every year. It accounts for a quarter of household waste, over five million tonnes annually, and as much again is generated during the transport process.

Packaging is important when food has to travel long distances. More than half of this is plastic. Plastic is made from oil, a valuable resource. It doesn't break down very easily in the ground and is challenging to recycle. There are over fifty different types of plastic, some of which react badly with each other during reprocessing. Biodegradeable versions may use material from genetically modified plants, or compete with food crops. If these are added to the general waste stream, they complicate the sorting still further.

Buy fresh from local sources. Bring it home in a paper bag, which goes into your compost bin. Have milk delivered in glass bottles, which can be used over sixty times each. Take cloth bags on shopping trips to save on plastic carriers – there used to be 13 billion per year given out in the UK alone.

For household goods, especially kitchen and bathroom products, buy in bulk and refill your own containers. Avoid tins of aerosol fresheners and use incense, or grow scented plants such as lemon balm. Try using essential oils in place of over-packaged perfumes. For your own parcels, pack items with shredded paper or home-made popcorn (no syrup!). Use scraps of nice cloth to wrap presents instead of paper.

There are thousands of disposable products available for everyday life – biros, razors, lighters. Make the effort to find the refillable options. Rechargeable batteries save you money after only a few uses. Disposable nappies occupy up to half a million tonnes of landfill in Britain per year; look for alternatives.

Many low quality goods are also on offer. Although these are cheap, they do not last and cannot be fixed, so generate huge amounts of waste. We need to be able to find products that respond to good maintenance; well made items which last.

Take purchases seriously. If an item can't be repaired, choose an alternative product which can be. Try to source what you need locally. It is easier to take it back if it is faulty, or needs servicing. Read the instructions and look after your possessions.

Following the latest fashions can waste resources. Suddenly perfectly good items are discarded, though there are many ways to pass them on responsibly. There is a gap in the market here for durable design and timeless beauty.

Reduce, reuse, repair.... all these prevent waste being created in the first place. We need to regain a sense of value and an appreciation of quality. Well made and carefully maintained furniture, household items and clothes can be sold on or donated to support a charity. Many of these are able to repair items for resale.

Historically, very little was thrown away. Towns have always had rules about taking refuse away from their main living and working areas. Their waste heaps are important finds for archaeologists studying everyday life in times past.

As the population in this country grew, this strategy began to fail. Heaps had to become landfill sites. These occupy increasingly large areas, giving off toxic effluent, gases and stench. Though this remains an important means of waste disposal, alternatives were needed.

Burning this rubbish is another way of dealing with it, especially where the heat can be used to generate power. The conversion of waste to energy becomes more of an economic proposition as the cost of oil rises. Issues around incineration include emission control, especially of dioxins and polychlorinated dibenzofurans (PCDFs), the disposal of the toxic ash residue, and lorry traffic generated by these large sites. However, a well run facility can generate enough power to run both itself and tens of thousands of nearby homes.

Landfill and incineration both destroy a lot of potentially useful material. Keeping in mind the increasing scarcity of raw materials and the damage that extraction does to the environment, we need to move away from a linear system. Disposal and creation need to be linked through recycling.

This is the final option, where something is completely finished with. If you have a garden, or even enough room in your kitchen for a Bokashi bin, you can see for yourself how food waste is recycled into soil.

Other household waste needs to be collected, transported to a specialised facility and transformed into new raw materials. Recycling on the industrial scale needed to effectively reuse all our throw away waste is a fast developing industry with many challenges and complexities.

For example, the recent trend towards centralised sorting at large Materials Recovery Facilities means that glass is now compacted with other waste. Different colours are mixed and it is no longer suitable for making new bottles. This has reduced the value of glass waste. Firms which depended on a supply of quality glass 'cullet' are now struggling to pay the bank loan they had to take out to invest in their machinery.

Recyclate can be considered as a valuable community resource. Glass is heavy, attracting high transport costs. It could be collected separately and turned into new products at small factories closer to towns. The involvement of the whole community provides better commercial security. Paper, cardboard, cloth and a number of other items could also be dealt with at a more local level.

Dealing with plastic waste, on the other hand, generates harsher pollutants and requires more specialised equipment, thus a larger, more expensive facility. These need to draw raw material - used plastic – from a wider area in order to create the turnover necessary to finance a large operation.

Surveys comparing the energy footprint of plastic packaging with alternatives do not take these factors into account. They ignore the potential for small scale reclamation.

Most people will recycle from their kitchens but only half as many from bathrooms and bedrooms.

One ton of recycled plastic saves nearly 6,000 Kwh of energy, over 16 barrels of oil, nearly a hundred million Btu's of energy, and 30 cubic yards of landfill space. If everyone in Somerset recycled just one extra plastic shampoo bottle a year, this would save over 17 megawatt hours. Recycling one glass bottle saves enough energy to keep a low energy light bulb going for two nights. Recycled aluminium only uses 5% of energy needed to process the same amount from mined bauxite.

Every small increase in household recycling adds up to a huge saving in energy, significantly reducing the need for new power stations. Establishing a reliable waste stream encourages small businesses to get involved.

For every tonne of domestic waste, 6 tonnes are created by businesses. There is a growing understanding that this waste can be valuable as well as unsightly and sometimes toxic. Various policies have been created to manage the recycling and disposal involved. Landfill directives aim to reduce biodegradable waste going into landfill, and to minimise the impact of the process of decay on the environment.

Your informed consumer choices are important to support these initiatives. Due to the long term movements of the air and sea, pollution anywhere on the planet is going to affect us eventually, perhaps when we are less able to deal with it. Long transport chains are neither sustainable nor resilient.

We need to bring the processing of the waste we create closer to home, where it can be monitored and used as a resource.

Waste (and Recycling!) Resilience Plan

Reduce, repair, re-use, recycle

The energy cost of waste is another factor of modern life which is subsidised by cheap fossil fuels. Goods have to be manufactured, transported and disposed of. Closing the loop to cut out the transport is the resilient way forward.

If we are aware of the true cost of waste disposal, it will encourage more responsible buying practices. Processing recyclate and remanufacturing goods at home will boost our local economies.

- Take steps to reduce the amount of potential waste coming into your house.
- Find out if you can have milk delivered in bottles. Some firms will deliver in the evening. If you use plastic bottles, rinsing them out helps the sorting process by removing organic materials.
- Avoid disposables, buy refillables. Use a bag free vacuum cleaner and empty it in your compost bin.
- Recycle everything that is collected in your area, and from all the household bins, not just the main one. If everyone in Somerset recycled just one more plastic bottle a week, the annual energy saved would be equivalent to a quarter of the output of a nuclear power station.
- Learn what the recycling symbols on packaging mean.
- Research the recycling process for different materials – plastics, cloth, paper, metal. Recycle things that aren't collected on the doorstep.
- Buy in bulk and transfer smaller amounts to your own containers.
- Look for ease of repair by a small local firm as a feature when buying new goods.
- Organise, or take part in, a guided tour of a modern recycling plant.
- Could glass, paper or card be collected and processed in your area? How would that work?

Chapter Eleven

Communication

Talking is the most basic form of communication by which we can exchange detailed information. Once, your neighbours were the people you talked to most. In a modern urban community, you may not even know them.

This can make starting community projects in your area challenging.

The local shop and pub, if you have them, are good contact points, but with so much car use many will travel elsewhere to shop and socialise. Find a suitable meeting hall or room in your area. Compose and distribute leaflets explaining your idea for a community meeting or interest group. Use local notice boards, or laminate posters and put them up in places where your neighbours are likcly to see them.

Think about your message. Who is your target audience? What would you like your leaflet to achieve? Do you need to draw a map for directions? Add some pictures? Give contact details?

Keep it clear and simple. A large heading should state the main purpose such as 'Join the New Book Club'. Include the date, time and place. Without cluttering up the leaflet with too much text, add anything else which might attract people, such as guest speakers or refreshments.

There are a number of useful web based resources for a community. Find your Freecycle or Streetbank site to exchange goods. Join or start a local chat forum or Facebook page. Emailing notices of events can save time and money, though be aware that some people rarely engage with the Internet. Contact the local paper; many have a free 'What's On' page.

If you need to look for funding, any potential providers will insist on proof that your community supports the project. Take a petition round – this will give you an opportunity to explain about it, listen to concerns or ideas and let people feel included. Persuade others to get involved and form an organisation.

Thanks to modern technology, most of our communication today is done within a 'community of interest' rather than a geographical community. Work involves much use of telephones and emails, we chat to those with similar interests on social networking sites, have weekends away or attend events with people from all over the country.

We live in a 'small world' where at least one member of a social group will have 'long distance connections'. Thus groups are linked together and news can travel fast. You can use your networks to arrange contacts when visiting a foreign country, find work opportunities, solutions to practical problems. A huge amount of information not available locally can be accessed through the technology of communication.

Compared to travelling in person to contact people, the energy used to feed these networks is small. A meeting that takes place by video-conference uses an average of one hundredth as much energy as one in which participants took a flight so that they could sit down together. Replacing just one in four of those meetings by a video call could save as much power as the entire internet consumes

How would you work that out? You would need to take into account the energy needed to produce all the servers, computers, smartphones, factoring in how long they last before needing replaced. Then there is the energy consumed by phone masts, wi-fi transmitters and cloud storage devices. There are the huge data storage facilities where giant fans are employed to keep the machinery cool.

Considering all this, according to a study in California, the entire Internet runs on about 2% of the total global energy used each year. Other research puts the figure as high as 10%. Collecting the necessary data is difficult in this fast moving field, but all agree that there are ways to reduce this energy use.

Many servers, exchanges and relays can be powered by renewable energy – solar panels on the building roofs, windmills in the same area as masts. Currently, the batteries in base stations become depleted within an hour of mains power loss. The ability to top them up with sun or wind power would extend the functionality of the network in an emergency – exactly when it is needed most.

Apple's data centres already have their own solar panel installations and run on 100% renewables. Very basic technical developments in the way data is moved around can save energy. When Facebook shifted from interpreted PHP to compiled C, server use was cut by half.

Your iPhone does not use more power that your fridge, not even when all its back up systems are considered. It does not take more energy to stream a film to your computer than it does to print it onto a DVD and ship it to you. If you plan to watch a movie many times, it may be more economical to buy a DVD, as long as it is of good quality. The energy cost of streaming a film is repeated every time it is viewed.

A mobile phone and a laptop computer can easily be recharged using solar panels in conjunction with a 12 volt storage battery and a small inverter to change the electricity to 240 volts mains type power. They are low energy devices compared to an electric kettle. If you are not usually off grid, keep the battery charged. An ordinary leisure battery, as found in shops catering for holiday caravans, can top up mobile phones for several days, but most can only supply a single charge to a laptop before needing replenished themselves.

Although the electronic communication network is robust, in an emergency the mobile phone and internet networks can become overwhelmed by the volume of traffic, especially in the most troubled area. It's helpful to keep calls as short as possible. The authorities have the ability to restrict public access to networks in a serious situation

Landlines are more resilient than mobile phones. They use cables to transmit calls, not radio waves. An inverter and battery set-up will keep your cordless phone, which depends on mains electricity, operating in a power cut, but it's better to have an old style telephone handy. These plug directly into the telephone inlet and draw power from that. It will work as long as the phone system does. Test yours before you need it, and add its location to your emergency list.

Most of the landline system is well protected. The 'last mile' to your home is the most vulnerable. Wires can be broken, junction boxes flooded or cables stolen. In an emergency situation, your community could work together to identify where repairs may be needed.

Emergency public announcements will be made via radio or television, and through government websites. Make sure you have a portable radio, preferably analogue and with large batteries. Digital radios use far more battery power and will be abandoned by the authorities before analogue. For real resilience, use rechargeable batteries and charge them with your inverter.

The old fashioned analogue radios worked by sending a continuous stream of electrical signals. Although they were subject to a lot of interference from atmospheric disturbance, at least some of the information would get through. Analogue radios can increase their signal range by turning up the power.

Digital equipment sends a coded signal in segments. Interference will take out a whole block of the message. A weak signal may be lost entirely. The system struggles to distinguish background noise from voices. Although the sound quality achieved by a digital system is superior in ordinary circumstances, analogue is more resilient in emergencies.

The Radio Amateurs' Emergency Network (RAYNET) was formed in 1953 after radio amateurs took a lead role in emergency communications during severe flooding. They use VHF and UHF radios, hand held or mounted on vehicles. They also help out at large community events, which is a good way to engage with the group and consider becoming a member.

Deprived of all electronic communication, there are traditional methods of signalling to fall back on. You can spell out messages in Morse code. The dots and dashes can be sent using a flashing light, tapping on walls or even by smoke signal. If you can see the other person, the arm movements of semaphore stand for letters in a similar way.

Messages sent by these methods need to be very short. The Morse code for 'Help' is a useful one to learn so that you can identify a distress call. It consists of the letters S.O.S, which is easily signalled by three dots (short flashes) followed by three dashes (long flashes) then three dots again. Repeat the signal until you get a response or the emergency is over.

Even shorter messages can be conveyed to rescuers in the air. White cloth laid out on a large flat area of grass or tarmac makes an 'H' sign for helicopters who need to land. In a remote area, laying out a large sign on clear ground with any materials available will help rescuers to locate you.

The speed of communication has increased exponentially in recent decades. This is of great value in emergencies; a global response can be coordinated swiftly. In everyday affairs, though, the blizzard of information makes it hard to come to informed decisions.

Communication Resilience Plan

Here are ten steps you can take to broaden your communication base. Spend some time getting to know the people around you, especially if you would like to start a local project. Think about your community of interest as well. This may be spread out over a much wider area.

Relying on networks and electronic devices which could stop functioning in an emergency is not resilient. Learn how to send and receive important messages without them. What could you need to communicate, and how would you do this?

- Design a leaflet or poster advertising a community event. Find out where you could display information so that your neighbours will see it.

- Is there a pub, cafe or hall in your area where people can meet up to discuss issues or have fun?

- See if you can find locally based forums, Freecycle groups and Facebook pages where news and goods are   exchanged. You could pick up some bargains!

- What are you interested in? Are there clubs or groups of like-minded people? Maybe they hold events which you could attend.

- What ideas and skills can you share? How could you communicate these? Try joining Streetbank.

- Practise Morse code and semaphore. Kids like secret codes!

- Keep a phone which plugs directly into the wall inlet in case of power cuts.

- Have a plan for communicating with your family in an emergency where mobile phone use is restricted.

- Learn how to use solar panels, 12 volt batteries and inverters to create an emergency charging station for your phones, computers and radios. Pay attention to safety advice. Batteries can explode if misused and electricity can cause fires. Gain confidence with off-grid solutions before you have to depend on them.

- Make sure you have a portable FM (analogue) radio, either a wind up device or one powered by rechargeable batteries. Know how to find both your local radio station and BBC Four.

Chapter Twelve

Clothing

Textiles have many uses, but the most important in a country prone to cold wet weather is as clothing. The continual need to repair or replace gives this resource a lot of potential in supporting a community economy. We need to begin by paying the extra for quality products and to support local suppliers.

Everyone used to make their own clothes – once they even spun and wove the actual material from raw wool or vegetable fibres. Today we can just go out and buy well made clothes of fine cotton, soft wools or strong artificial materials – isn't life so much better?

Well, yes in many ways. Nothing could be worse than having to spend hours spinning or sewing if you don't enjoy it. It's an improvement to have dyes which don't run or fade, wonderful not to have to worry about the cost of the clothes your children ruin in play.

But a huge amount of the toxic agricultural chemicals used in the world are for growing cotton. We learn that cheap clothing is made through exploiting families out of sight in other countries. It costs less than a penny to ship a cheap shirt to the UK; meanwhile British farmers can't sell their wool because not enough people are prepared to pay extra for local produce.

Currently 5% of the global carbon footprint of the UK relates to clothing, and about 7% of our total water footprint. Almost 90% of this water is used overseas; more than half in lands already short of water. With growing populations pressuring their reserves, this method of production may become far more expensive. We should cultivate fibre plants such as hemp, flax and nettle here instead, and make more use of wool.

You can help to create a market for local resources by buying fabrics which could potentially be sourced here. We would be more aware of the waste generated in production, control any pollutants and manage the water use. The energy used in transport would be greatly reduced. Money would circulate closer to home.

Explore the use of local materials. Does your area support sheep? Could flax be grown there? Are there factories which need to dispose of scrap cloth?

Spinning and knitting can be revived, using wool from organically reared sheep to make socks and good thick jumpers. Begin with raw wool, either from a bought fleece or gathered from hedges while out walking. This will need to be washed and combed, or carded.

Wool can also be bought ready for spinning. It's not essential to have a spinning wheel. You can use a simple drop spindle as seen in Egyptian tomb paintings, made from a long pencil and an old CD. Spun wool is expensive, so it is worth making your own if you can. Learn to knit; there are instructions and patterns in books or on the internet. It's helpful to go to a class or join a group and share experiences.

Synthetic fibres, such as nylon, polyester and acrylic, are made using oil as a raw material. They are easy to care for, but are more flammable than natural fibres. Their manufacture generates toxic waste and the microfibres shed when washing are a major pollution hazard.

Such microfibres account for over half of the plastic in the oceans. They are tiny enough to enter the living cells of marine life, which we then eat. Cells containing these plastic fragments may not function properly; the subject is still under study.

Semi-synthetic cloth such as viscose rayon is made from the cellulose in wood pulp, so it is far less dependent on petroleum supplies. It requires factory processing and makes use of a toxic oil based solvent. Properly managed, however, over 98% of this can be recovered and reused. Rayon can be blended with natural fibres and is very versatile. It can be turned into industrial yarn for conveyor belts or blended with silk for dresses. A type of rayon is manufactured in the UK, in Grimsby.

Although cheap clothes are tempting, the quality is often poor. Handmade garments are more expensive than imported factory produce, but last longer and can be repaired. Learn how to look for quality; check the seams and stitching before you buy. Find out which brand labels have a name for style and durability; look for these in second hand shops.

Conserve your good clothes. Then you can afford to buy the organically grown and locally sourced fabrics which support resilience. Linen is very hard wearing. Hemp and nettles are cheap to grow, requiring little or no agrochemicals.

Invest in clothes to be worn when in town or at work. Keep these in good condition. At home, when gardening or just staying in, have a set of loose, hardwearing clothes, ideally made of hemp.

Change into your good clothes to go out, change back once at home and air used clothes over the back of a chair. Wash them with care and only when they have been worn on several occasions. Thus they will last longer. If it is cold, wear thin, easily washed leggings and vests as under layers.

Clothes are often thrown away because they no longer fit. You could have them adjusted; shops could help with access to repair and alteration services. Learn to sew buttons, darn woollen jumpers and socks, fix zips and restyle old clothes. Maybe one of your neighbours is particularly good at this.

Expensive clothes can be repaired using 'Invisible Mending'. This involves taking individual threads from a concealed part of the garment and weaving them over the damaged area. Depending how the item was damaged, this cost may even be met by your household insurance. There is a specialist shop in London appropriately named 'The Old Invisible Mending Shop'.

For most people, value for money is the main factor in choosing clothes. Only a fifth say the latest trends influence them. Manufacturers could create more versatile styles, source fabrics closer to home and support clothes care. Buy-back schemes have been well received; you must have kept the garment in good condition.

Well cared for clothes can also be passed around your family, sold on-line or swapped. Currently, most clothes last about two years. Making them last longer saves money and energy. More people would use second hand clothes if a bigger range were available.

Damage in the wash accounts for much loss. Read and follow the care instructions for your clothes. Try using lower temperatures and avoid harsh chemical detergents. Environmentally friendly products such as ecoballs and soap nuts have favourable reviews from users. If you live in a hard water area, use a regular soap powder from time to time to avoid build up of limescale in your machine.

It has been estimated that, although we spend hundreds of pounds a year on clothes, a third of our wardrobe has not been used for over a year. Many people send old clothes to landfill unaware of the extent to which they can be recycled and the significant amount of energy this saves.

Fabric is not just for clothes but also for household items such as bedding, carpets and curtains.

The finely woven sheets and quilt covers available today have to be made by machines, which use energy. Currently, most of this is from fossil fuels, but large scale renewables are capable of powering entire factories. We can access the energy of tides and waves all around our island. Although Britain isn't as well endowed with sunlight as other lands, there is plenty of wind and running water.

Bedding used to be cared for and repaired. Sheets were 'turned'; cut down the middle where there is most wear and sewn back together with the worn sections on the outside. Some people could even achieve a smooth darn to repair holes, especially in linen sheets. These were so hard wearing that they used to be mentioned in peoples' wills!

Try reading reviews on-line to see if you can find brand names with a reputation for quality bedding.

Modern fitted carpets are also machine made, and very helpful in reducing domestic heat loss. Alternatives, such as wooden floors with solar powered underfloor heating, will take time to develop. The recent floods, however, remind us that our ancestors were on to something with their stone floors and movable rugs.

Curtains are essential for home insulation too. They are your 'face to the world' so it is worth making them attractive. Replace plastic rails as they break with wooden ones.

There's scope for many useful creative skills with fabrics. If you enjoy quilting or patchwork, why not collect pieces of cloth as souvenirs of holidays and special occasions to incorporate into your work? Rag rugs can be very decorative, only needing recycled cloth and sacking as materials.

Most of these crafts are ideal for filling in long winter evenings at home. The materials and tools you need are cheap and accessible. It's a good place to start.

Clothing (and Fabrics) Resilience Plan

Here are ten steps you can take. You may be following some of these suggestions already. Although each action seems small and insignificant, taken across the whole country they add up to huge savings in energy and resources.

- Make sure all your old clothing and fabric gets recycled.
- Seek alternatives to cotton and synthetic fibres when buying clothes.
- Learn basic sewing – how to replace buttons, adjust simple hems, darn woollen socks.
- Find out how to identify quality in clothes and see what you can get second hand.
- Look after your clothes in the wash. Sort loads, use less of the harsh chemical detergents, air clothes after wearing to cut down on washing.
- Take your shoes off when you come home, and change into slippers or soled socks. This will extend the life of your carpets. Grit from the street is a major cause of wear.
- Find a local person who can make a good job of tricky repairs such as zips. Ask them to help you identify features which make garments easier to fix. Could they restyle some of your older clothes?
- Is there a sewing or knitting circle in your area? You could exchange ideas and build up a clothes swap shop.
- Study types of material and learn which ones could be grown or processed in your area.
- Learn a skill – spinning, knitting, weaving, crochet, rug making – and make useful household items from raw materials.

Much of the energy use and waste around clothing production happens during manufacture. If consumer trends move away from cheap throwaway clothes, industry will have to change in response.

By looking after your clothes and making them last longer, you can afford to buy quality and support **Local Businesses.** Paying attention to how you do your laundry will reduce **Water** pollution and the associated costs. Wearing warmer clothes indoors means you can turn your heating thermostat down and save **Energy.**

Chapter Thirteen

Environment

What do you see when you look out of your window at home, work or school? That is your environment. Earth and air are its main features. Sometimes you can see water as well. It has weather, landscape and various creatures existing without the permission of humans.

You may live among the lights and action of a city centre, or out in the countryside where the stillness of the view is only broken by the gently turning windmills. The natural environment is struggling to survive in both.

The environment not only sustains nature but provides all of our resources, including living space. Its welfare is closely linked to social and economic demands. If too many people rely on the cnvironment for their basic needs, resources cannot regenerate fast enough and the eco-system is soon depleted.

The extraction of minerals and fossil fuels creates widespread damage, and it is often many years before productivity of any kind can be returned to the region. Industrial farming destroys soil quality and causes erosion. The polluted silt that was once topsoil clogs the waterways.

More violent storms are predicted for the British Isles in coming years, with significantly wetter winters and drier summers. If sea levels rise, this will impact on coastal cities and on major agricultural areas such as East Anglia. The Fens produce nearly 40% of England's field grown vegetables.

The increasing global competition for resources is also likely to affect us. Some data indicates that humans are now living beyond the carrying capacity of the entire planet – the maximum population size that the environment can hold.

Few developed countries are able to sustain themselves on their own resources. The last time Britain could feed its own people was in 1830. Europe as a whole does better. It is largely self-sufficient in grains, oils, sugar and meat. Animal feed, however, is nearly all imported.

Finding the carrying capacity of the British Isles is difficult. Most sources avoid the problem through denial. The most realistic period to look at for information are the years just after WWII. With a population of about 47 million, we were very nearly self-sufficient. Fossil fuel use was conserved, and the soil was still healthy.

Since then housing, infrastructure and pollution has covered a lot of productive land. The population in 2012 was nearly 64 million, and rising. Technological 'miracles' designed to 'feed the world' turn out to solve short term problems while making the long term situation worse.

In 2011 the International Resource Panel hosted by the United Nations Environment Programme warned that, projecting from current figures for growth, the global rate of consumption will treble by the year 2050. Resource wars have already broken out and are likely to increase, mainly over fossil fuels, water and food.

Despite the political and religious pressures against the concept, countries need to acknowledge their carrying capacity and begin to work with it. We cannot maintain a cowardly reliance on conflict or natural disaster to restore the balance. The disruption would release too many toxins which we have created and now need to look after.

According to the Bruntland Commission of the United Nations in 1987: 'sustainable development is development that meets the needs of the present without compromising the ability of future generations to meet their needs.'

The aim of sustainable practices is to imitate healthy biological systems. These are diverse, resilient and productive over time despite cycles of peaks and scarcity. New methods of agriculture are emerging, such as permaculture and forest gardening, which can maximise productivity for a given area using organic means.

Permaculture, or permanent agriculture, uses the natural tendencies of the prevailing ecosystem in designing cultivation. Different types of food plants are often mixed together, which makes them harder for pests to find. If disease attacks one crop, there are others to rely on. Friendly insects are encouraged and the landscape as a whole is pleasant to the eye.

Members of the community gather vegetables as they are needed, preserving or trading their small seasonal surpluses. It is difficult to engage a resilient system like this with centralised food distribution. In a monoculture field, the estimated yield can be used as security for a bank loan. With land under permaculture, the criteria for success is feeding the local community.

The use of machinery on farmland compacts the soil and ruins its structure. In a permaculture system, there is very little call for this, and the labour involved in maintaining productivity is not arduous. They do take time to develop, but anyone can begin to apply the basic principles to a garden or allotment.

Farmers and small holders could have more hedges maintained using traditional laying rather than flailing; this practice has cost us hundreds of species of plants and insects. Large fields of a single crop are not the best use of land for either food production or wildlife. Smaller, diverse farms are far more resilient. With a local market for produce, money could be invested in these techniques, providing yet more employment as well as enhancing the natural environment.

When applying chemical fertilisers, only nitrogen, potassium and phosphorous are considered. Many other trace minerals, such as zinc and magnesium, can be depleted to a level where the plants are visibly sick before the imbalance is addressed. These plants are less able to resist disease and pests, so need the help of pesticides. Even then, there are organic alternatives to malathion and other toxic chemicals.

Once, the land, rivers and sea seemed to be infinitely capable of exploitation, but after decades of ugly and dangerous pollution, we are making efforts to clean it up and to restrict the practices of industry. After the ignorance and excesses of the Industrial Revolution, we have realised that mental health depends on access to natural beauty.

Unfortunately the response of many larger companies was to take advantage of globalisation and move operations to 'under polluted' countries. It was cheaper to make goods abroad and ship them back to Britain than to exercise a responsible attitude to pollution.

The rising cost of fuel and other factors, such as piracy, make this option less attractive now. Modern companies are more likely to be looking at reducing the resources needed to produce, consume and dispose of a unit of stuff. Better design and more advanced technology are used. The Internet, particularly social networking, reveals bad practice to home customers, who are becoming increasingly influenced by quality and ethics rather than price.

New urban areas need to incorporate green infrastructure. Circular flow land use management is aimed at reducing urban sprawl and restoring green areas by prioritising inner city development. Roof space can be used for solar panels or gardens with bee hives.

Long lived, healthy wetlands and forest are important, particularly to drainage and flood prevention in a small wet island like ours. These need to be restored as well as protected. Using permaculture design ideas, changes in water management strategies would result in productive land at each stage. Grant funding may be required to support this process until public awareness creates a market for the produce.

For example, the Somerset levels used to be an important supplier of willow for baskets. This market disappeared as plastic and cardboard packaging took over. The willow was cut down and replaced by grass fields. These do not retain water in the same way, leading to major floods.

The accompanying storms blew down many garden fences made from solid panels. Fences made from woven willow allow air to pass through them and are better able to resist wind. If people were prepared to adjust their buying habits, it would support the change in agriculture required to prevent their houses being flooded.

Willow can take up toxins from the soil, cleaning it ready for food production. There is a lot of research around this subject, particularly looking at the possible role of fungi. Some species of these are capable of thriving on chemical spills or even radioactive land.

Although resilience depends upon micromanaging local resources, the resilient community must look out to the larger picture as well. Globalisation has profited the few at the expense of the many, and is now unable to maintain its promises. We have simply run out of globe to exploit.

The concept of 'decoupling' is being studied in economic fields. An economy that can maintain GDP growth without increasing negative pressure on the environment is said to be 'decoupled'. How this can be achieved is the subject of much debate.

Moving away from generating all money as debt to private banks, with interest payments eternally added such that only through continual growth can the debt be serviced, would surely help. There are other valid models for a working economy, and gross domestic product may not be the most meaningful way of measuring success.

Environment Resilience Plan

- Pay attention to the welfare of wildlife in your area. Feed the birds. Try not to acquire a cat.
- If you have a garden, avoid the use of chemicals. Practise not walking on the soil. Feel the difference after it has recovered. If you don't have a garden, a balcony or windowbox can support many bee-friendly flowers.
- Visit an organic farm, a forest garden, a permaculture grower. Try to visit an intensive livestock farm. These are less welcoming. Look at the waste produced and the living conditions. Do you think you would be able to stay healthy here?
- Plant a nut tree. They take a long time to mature. A walnut won't produce nuts until it is 25 years old.
- Take an interest in development around you and lobby for more sustainable features in each plan.
- Learn about your local environment, study its history and the way resources have been used.
- Ask questions.
- Where does money come from? Where does it go? What can you do to make it stay in your area? How would that benefit you? Why do rents and mortgages cost about the same each week?
- How does a debt-based economy work and what are the alternatives?
- If you could design a 200 year plan to reduce the population of the British Isles to 45 million, while retaining an acceptable quality of life for everyone and moving towards self-sufficiency in essentials, what would it look like?

Interlude One

The **Resources** quadrant of the Resilience Wheel is where you can make most progress as an individual.

An understanding of key resources is important basic knowledge when considering how to move forward, to design a strategy, or to assess a current position.

Reflect for a moment on your personal resilience plan.

Think about each of the nine sections under **Resources**.

You may already be following some of the suggestions. The first few given are quite easy, even becoming mainstream as more people engage with sustainable lifestyles. Further down each list, the actions become more challenging. You can use these lists to help calibrate your 'Resilience Score' in each section, from 1 – 10 as described in Chapter Three.

Appendix One contains a full Resilience Assessment based on these tasks. You can calculate your current practical resilience and express it as a percentage of the basic ideal. Further work on the recommended actions will increase your score in a measurable way.

These Resilience Plans cover actions which are all achievable in Britain. Some elements will need to be slightly adapted for different locations. As the tasks are designed to lead on to further levels of practical resilience, don't depart too far from the originals. Their direction may not be immediately clear.

This book is written from the perspective of a market town in Somerset, a largely rural county of Britain. Urban areas face different types of challenge around **food** and **waste**. There are more commercial opportunities and better **transport** links. City dwellers will find some aspects of their resilience plan easier than people in rural areas do; with other parts, the reverse will be the case.

The climate of these islands is generally cool and wet. There is a well established infrastructure and a long coastline. Some or all of these features may not apply in other countries.

The principles of practical resilience are universal. If you live in Mexico City, you still need **clothing**. It still has to come from somewhere, somehow. The residents of Tokyo need **energy** for lighting. In the Sahara desert, you will certainly need **water**. Everyone needs **communication** to come to group decisions.

Look at where you live. Study the history of resource use in your immediate area, your administrative district, your country as a whole. What has been tried in the past? Where did it end up? What failed and what succeeded?

Don't get caught up in the bigger picture though. Just glance at it for ideas on direction. Check which raw materials could be sourced locally, whether they currently are or not. Are there luxury items – a type of cheese, a style of cloth, a variety of fruit – associated with your area?

Among the many benefits of following a Resilience Plan is greater awareness of your personal role in your environment.

No matter where you are, the Resilience Wheel can be used as a framework to analyse your current position and to evolve strategies for progress. Remember that resilience starts at ground level and works up. Ultimately, an informed population drives policy decisions.

The central goal is to be independent of global events in the supply of your absolute basic needs. When things go well in the world, there will be a lively international exchange of various goods – coffee, gadgets, medicines, craft items, exotic foods and so on. If things go badly, this may diminish, but at least you can survive to trade another day.

Although we are far from resilient on this island, we still have the use of fossil fuel energy for a while longer. Peak oil does not mean that supplies will immediately dry up, just that we need to start working on an exit strategy. Political uncertainty in the global arena indicates that sooner rather than later would be good.

Resources are of immediate, visible concern. There's been a lot of work already on how they can be managed sustainably. Clear paths can be found which lead to significant positive changes. The resilience plan is mapped out. You only need to follow it.

Now we move into less well-charted territory with **Reskilling**.

In an industrialised society, almost all the stuff surrounding you is made in a factory. The core processes by which raw materials are transformed into useful objects are obscure. Most people couldn't qualify for a place in the Stone Age.

Yet the ability to mass produce was built up over time. The discoveries of certain key chemicals and basic mechanical processes were important features. These discoveries were made by people who could access only the most basic technology.

It's not impossible to create smaller, community based factories and workshops which could continue to provide the goods we take for granted in this current era of cheap fossil fuel energy.

It's not going to be easy either.

Let's take a look at **Reskilling**.

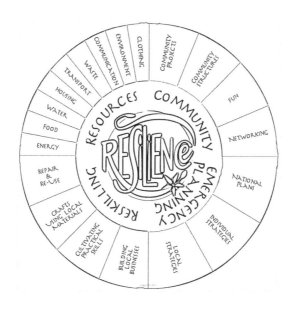

Chapter Fourteen

Introduction to Re-Skilling

The Resources section of the Resilience Wheel covers the necessities of life. Individual actions add up to make big differences here. You can act alone, or just within your own household. To move further into practical resilience, however, one must start to engage with others.

Not so long ago, most people were accustomed to use a variety of tools, and knew how to repair them. This knowledge is becoming rarer, and must be recovered. Hence the term 're-skilling' began to be used by the Transition movement to describe this process.

For example, as you are cultivating your allotment, you find your tools need sharpening. A rake handle breaks. Your strimmer becomes jammed. Sooner or later, there will be a limit to the number of crafts you can learn personally, especially since many require tuition or practice to make a decent job.

Decisions around resource use can be taken quickly, and within the existing framework. It takes time to learn practical skills. In the resilience plan for this quadrant, each step will have to be covered in more detail. New ground has to be created to move forward on.

Rural areas used to be self sufficient in manufactured goods as well as food. Within easy reach, there would be blacksmiths, potters, spinners and weavers, wood carvers and furniture makers, leather workers and many more. All these people would be able to fix items as well as make new ones. It was not a throwaway culture. Even a small local economy supported many skilled craftspeople who were respected by their communities and could take pride in their daily work.

A lot of these trades survived the move to towns and cities at first, but the Industrial Revolution with its mechanised production lines and cheaper goods eventually undermined them and gradually many crafts disappeared. The commercial production of cloth in rural areas declined in competition with the huge textile mills. The advent of the motor car finally put an end to the blacksmiths and harness makers, who had survived longer than most.

Even then, there used to be a shed and a vegetable patch in most gardens. Craft work, including repairs, is best done as part of a community. Feedback and the exchange of ideas facilitates learning. The garden shed was more than just a storage space. Many people had extensive collections of tools. Some created complex models as a hobby. Advice and skill sharing networks grew up over years, sometimes spanning generations.

The social upheaval of the nineteen-sixties, with mass movement into new housing schemes and geographical relocation destroyed this web of competence. Before it had time to regrow into the empty space, its place had been taken by throwaway goods. The difficult process of getting to know new people could be short-circuited by spending money.

Practical skills were once part of life. Now, even gardening is becoming a lost art.

We are used to a lifestyle with minimal effort. Flick a switch, turn on a tap and things happen, as if we had the genie of the magic lamp at our service. The long process of learning and applying a skill has become irrelevant to fulfilling our needs.

Relatively few people in this country are able to make or fix everyday household items. Technology has been directed at the manufacture of disposable goods with sealed workings which cannot be repaired. Fashion dictates that mending is scruffy and a sign of poverty.

While some of our various gadgets may indeed be too complex to fix, there are still a lot of everyday items which could be made or repaired at home or locally. A resilient community needs to rediscover these skills and adapt them to modern life.

Making things from raw materials can be more complex than it seems. A wooden ladder looks like a simple item to make. However, it needs to be strong, and resistant to rot caused by water, as it will be used outside. The rungs were always made of heart of oak, never sawn into shape as this weakened the grain of the wood and allowed damp in. Instead, they were split into the rough shape and trimmed using a draw knife. Rungs were oval, not round, for extra strength. The uprights were ash or cedar. Care was taken not to split these when hammering the rungs into place. Thin iron bracing rods at intervals prevented the ladder falling apart.

Every craft draws on this sort of detailed understanding of materials, tools and the purpose of the finished item. This knowledge is best learned and passed on while actually working. Even instructional videos can only go so far, and are unlikely to be accessible in a survival situation anyway.

Traditional crafts are dying out as the last practitioners retire. People need to take them on as hobbies in order to keep the skills alive, even if there is little call for them while we still have technology.

Once, you would expect to live in the same county all your life, even working at the same job. There was continuity. Now, one may change an entire career several times, move from one end of the country to the other and back according to whim or need. Stagnation can be avoided, but a sense of cohesive purpose can be hard to find.

A real craft can provide a theme to modern lives. Find one which suits you and explore it fully. Join a group with similar interests. Collect appropriate tools, learn the raw materials. Choose holiday destinations which relate to it in some way.

If you have to leave your identity as an insurance salesman in Norfolk behind to become a bus driver in Powys, it may be disorientating. You'll have to get to know different people, to find a place in a new community. Very little of your old knowledge and experience will be helpful. Your identity is in danger of being only defined by others.

A craft is something that travels with you.

"As the huge multinational corporations close in on the world, fewer and fewer individuals find themselves in the position of being able to produce anything of use or beauty themselves – they are all just cogs in some huge money-making machine with its head office thousands of miles away and God knows where!

Apart from the fact that this huge global monstrosity is not sustainable and is due to come crashing down anyway, the intolerable aridness and boredom for most people will eventually become unbearable and we will all rebel. We will seize the right again to make things of utility and beauty for ourselves, with our own intelligence and our own hands, helped by simple, basic and, so often beautiful, tools"

John Seymour
'The Forgotten Arts and Crafts', Dorling Kindersley 2001

Chapter Fifteen

Re-use and Repair

Re-using and repairing discarded goods saves on energy and resources. The problem is to link people who need to get rid of sound items with those who are looking for such an item, or are willing to collect and repair as a business or service.

You've got something which isn't fit for purpose any more. In a throwaway culture you would simply dump it in landfill, or add it to the hoard in the attic and buy a new one, but now we need to look at alternative solutions.

Is it still working, or in good condition? There are websites and social media platforms where you can buy and sell used items. People who are able to work at home may make a small income from trading on these sites. If you can't find the time to do this yourself, they could sell for you, charging a small commission.

Selling through large Internet sites can reach a lot of customers but the various costs, postage and time which needs to be spent can reduce your profit, especially if you only use the service rarely. There may be a Facebook page or chat forum devoted to a market closer to home. Goods can be dropped off locally and there are no fees.

Avoid the Internet completely? Try placing cards in local shops. See if there are free small ads in your local paper. If you have the space, invite your neighbours to a garage sale. A major clear out can be followed by a stall at your local car boot sale. Check the weather forecast first!

If you can't sell an item, or it's not worth bothering to try, you can give it away. The Freecycle network is formed of small groups across the world. You join their forum and offer goods by email. They have to be free. People contact you and a collection time is arranged. Once the item has gone, you should post a 'Taken' message.

Freecycle is worth checking first if you need something; furniture, garden supplies, toys. You can see what is on offer, or post a 'Wanted' message. Learn to plan purchases in advance. This gives you time to find options which support resilience.

Some charitable organisations have the space and equipment to refurbish goods through cleaning and servicing. The Furniture Re-use Network is a good place to find these people. They support more than 300 charities, with the aim of reducing both poverty and waste.

In many areas, the local Council, or community groups, run re-use and repair schemes. Some target businesses as well as individuals. The Halls of Residence Re-use Scheme works with the management and students in universities. Outgoing students donate unwanted goods such as bedding, books and kitchen equipment to the scheme. Over 90% of these items can be saved from landfill. Most are donated to charities or sold for a nominal sum to the incoming students.

Does your item need repair? Would you carry on using it if it worked again? There are many places on-line where you can source spare parts for household goods or learn repair techniques. Keep the original instructions in a safe place. You may need to know the make and model.

Remember to find out how easily something can be repaired before you buy it. Learn about basic fixtures and fittings, explore the difference between engineered products, like MDF, and real wood. Hinges should be basic folding ones. Avoid parts made of plastic. It can be moulded into many slightly different shapes so that you can never find quite the right one for a repair. Plastic parts are difficult to duplicate with more accessible materials.

The Repair Cafe movement, founded in Holland, supports free meeting spaces with tools and advice where people can fix their stuff together. They don't compete with professionals – advising people to go to an expert where necessary – but aim to encourage the concept of not throwing things away.

Experienced crafts people and people with broken items mix in a friendly atmosphere. The ability to repair, so quickly lost, is valued. Practical skills are passed on. Their website gives the location of hundreds of these cafes across Europe; they are especially popular in Germany. It isn't necessary to have a full time cafe to start a branch in your area. You can use a community hall. The Repair Cafe organisation will help you set one up for a small fee if you want to be part of their group.

As an individual, you can begin by acquiring a basic repair kit for household items.

Useful tools to have

For furniture repair and other woodworking projects:-
- a hammer
- a saw
- a drill, even a hand drill is useful and, at worst, you can improvise with an awl for making small holes.
- a large screwdriver
- a medium sized one for most indoor jobs
- a small one for electrical items, so that you can at least change batteries.
- a tape measure, spirit level, knife and sharpening stone for the really ambitious.

You should have both a flat bladed and a cross head screwdriver in each size. They can be used for metalwork as well. You'll also need a hacksaw and a pair of wire cutters there.

Machinery requires spanners of exact sizes and you may need to team up with someone who knows enough about it to possess a set. At the very least, they can match known sizes to the nuts on your bicycle or lawn mower so that you can go and buy your own spanners.

Another important tool is a set of Allen keys. You'll need these about once every two years, mainly to dismantle flat pack furniture. No other tool can do the job, so remember where you put them. The flat pack furniture will have come with its own key, which will be in a safe place somewhere, possibly in the house of the previous owner.

Landlords of today often discourage DIY repairs by their tenants. Some refuse to allow so much as a picture hook to be put up. If you need shelf space, try adapting an old wardrobe. Natural wood, even plywood, is a far better material to work with than fibreboards. Learn about glues, paints and varnish.

A sewing kit is another basic piece of equipment. Ideally, it is kept in a tin to discourage the pins and needles from escaping into the carpet. Apart from those, it needs scissors which fit in the tin, a selection of cottons in the colours you are most likely to use, and whatever odds and ends might come in useful, such as spare buttons.

Cotton thread should be used with natural textiles, and polyester with manmade cloth. Woollen socks can be darned, using a needle thick enough to be threaded with wool. Once, a wooden darning mushroom would have been an essential item in every sewing kit. The curved surface helped keep the shape of the sock heel as it was repaired. The stem was often hollow, to hold the special needles.

At the other end of the scale, the energy savings of re-use and repair translate into industrial amounts of money. The profit motive, backed by a number of government directives on waste, has inspired some major progress.

Industrial Re-use

When something is recycled, it is broken down into its component materials which are used to make different products. The re-use or repair of whole products saves more energy. It is of growing importance in industry, where it often involves re-manufacturing. The used item is returned to the guaranteed level of performance it had when new.

Large machinery- jet engines, pumps, factory equipment – is often overhauled and resold. Car spares, tyres, printer cartridges and computers can be re-manufactured. This saves up to 85% of the energy required to create the items from raw materials. The industry as a whole is worth nearly £5 billion to the British economy.

Currently over 90% of uniforms and corporate clothing is discarded. Businesses can apply for grant funding for repair and re-use initiatives, or access advice on the full environmental impact when choosing materials. Their buying power could make a real difference to local fibre growers and textile manufacturers.

Re-use and Repair Resilience Plan

Take care when trying to repair things powered by mains electricity. Always disconnect them from the power source, even if you are only unjamming garden tools.

Beware of components called capacitors. These store electricity, and can give you a nasty shock even when a device is turned off. Warnings about not dismantling outer casings may mean one of these is lurking inside. Try to find a local repair service for electrical and gas appliances.

- Put yourself in charge of when you choose to buy a new item. Buy quality to last and to be repairable. Stop being a passive victim of planned obsolescence!
- Join Freecycle, look for other places on-line where you can access local exchange of goods and services.
- Find a holiday destination with a Repair Cafe nearby, visit for a cup of tea and see what's going on. Check on-line for their opening days.
- Learn how to do your basic repairs. Specialise in one to 'skill swap' with.
- Cultivate a different sort of awareness. Look at the things around you and think about where they came from. How resilient are they?
- The next time something of yours breaks, consider how it could be fixed.
- If it can't be fixed, consider replacing it with something which can be.
- If it can't be replaced with something which can be fixed, consider doing without it.

Chapter Sixteen

Cultivating Practical Skills

Between work, socialising and television, there may seem to be little time left for developing a skill. There's no need to be too ambitious at first though; gardening and cooking can be extended into productive hobbies.

These essential skills are a good place to start. Both require tools. Learn the purposes of these, why they make the task easier, how to maintain them in a useful condition. Quality tools are not throwaway items. Acquire a habit of respect for them.

Cookery is underestimated as a craft. The ability to fashion elaborate and complicated dishes is only one aspect of it. There is plenty of scope for the reluctant cook to minimise time spent in the kitchen, while not resorting to processed foods. A roast dinner followed by stew and soup takes care of half the week. Use your own vegetables, gathered from the allotment at the weekend. The whole family can get involved with preparing enough for all three meals.

Growing food leads into the science of soil quality, plant nutrition and pest control. Does woad, hemp or flax flourish in your area? Grow some and find out. Plant a small square of wheat and grind the grain as a project. How much flour do you get?

Read about permaculture. Can you apply any of the techniques to your garden? You could make your own flowerpots; will they crack if it gets too cold? How can you prevent this?

Find a short pottery course, or a craft event offering hands-on experience. Learning an advanced skill takes time and patience. Pick something that is relevant to your basic needs and explore it for a year. Although much can be learned from books and on-line, spending time with a teacher is important. Assiduous practising is far better than buying expensive equipment.

If you don't feel you can progress in a craft after a reasonable attempt, choose another. The lopsided pots and rather odd clay sculptures prove that at least you tried. Meanwhile, you have become quite good at fixing broken garden tools, so you study woodwork instead.

Your neighbours bring their tools to be fixed. You start taking an interest in metalworking as well. People talk about your skill. A community business initiative offers you premises....

Striking a balance between daydreaming and focus is important with craftwork, especially if it involves sharp tools. Making something new using your hands often involves at least one stage of repetitive actions. Once you have achieved basic competence in the techniques, your mind tends to drift into relaxing reverie.

Although this is an important part of the creative process, a level of alertness must be kept. Unravelling rows of knitting done in the wrong pattern, or shaving too much off a crucial piece of wood will soon bring this home. Allowing yourself to brood on problems is more likely to result in spoiled work. Redirect your thoughts into imagining how the finished product will look.

It will probably not be as perfect as the examples in glossy magazines or on television. Remember the media can pick images from the best craftspeople in the world. Comparison with these has been a discouraging influence on amateurs for decades.

Competition with machine made goods is also difficult. Little skill or thought goes into factory produce, yet it looks good and costs less. It lacks creative imagination and individual meaning though. The bowls you turned from the old cherry tree which grew in your grandmother's garden are uniquely part of your life.

Woodworking can be a pleasant and productive hobby. Even if you lack space, you could learn to carve utensils and ornaments, make delicate inlaid boxes or driftwood sculptures. If you can work outside, there is basketry, garden furniture and many other avenues to explore. Learn about trees, source British wood, know the history of the pieces you make.

Outside is the best place for the noisier or messier crafts such as stoneworking, pottery and blacksmithing. You would need the use of a workshop, either your own or one belonging to your community, to develop these skills. Once they were on display in every village, as part of ordinary life. Today it requires a dedicated effort to provide young people with the chance to experience them.

Opportunities still exist to explore crafts. Use the kitchen to create practical everyday items, while listening to the radio. Label craft materials carefully and store them away from food. Keeping PVA glue in an old mayonnaise jar beside the salt is asking for trouble. Some mix ups can even be dangerous.

Recipes for herbal ointments, bath products and cleaning materials are easily obtained from books or the Internet. Bath bombs and salts can be made at home for yourself or as presents. Soap making is more challenging; the process will dissolve most metal utensils. Employ pyrex, stainless steel or ceramics, and be sure to let the soap cure for several weeks before using.

Twigs, pine cones, dried leaves and flowers are the ingredients for pot pourri. Grow them in the garden, collect them on a family walk. Dry out the mix and layer it in a bowl with rock salt, which absorbs unwanted smells. Add a few drops of essential oils; no more packaged and chemical room fresheners!

Wine making is generally popular with the community. Gather wild fruits, avoiding those near main roads, or take advantage of seasonal surpluses. Jams, chutneys, pickles and flavoured vinegars are other spin offs from growing food.

Then there are the various textile crafts. Knitting and crochet can take some time to master, but are easily done at home, on public transport, or among friends. Weaving and spinning are less mobile. Domestic sewing machines allow the expert user to fashion quality clothes from fabric, individually tailored.

As a craft is developed, more complicated tools are often needed. Other members of the community would engage with a craftsperson to make and repair these. Blacksmiths were the most important resource. They could produce metal parts to order, such as hooks and fastenings. This was a highly skilled job and survived well into the Industrial Revolution. In some remote areas of the world, functioning engine parts can still be copied from a broken original.

Carpenters made wheels, ladders and weaving looms as well as furniture. There was a great deal of knowledge about how to join pieces of wood effectively, which is now being lost. The type of wood used for various purposes is important. Some, like yew, are not suitable for food containers. Some, like hickory, are especially good for tool handles.

Crafting the fine angles needed for wagon wheel parts is a dying art, as is that of making waterproof barrels. Without our constant supply of factory made or imported goods, we could be reduced to a crude and primitive level very quickly. Most of us don't even know how to make stone tools. Supporting heritage crafts by learning a skill is good for personal self-development, but also a vital means of keeping them alive for community resilience.

Using tools for simple repairs around the house encourages a wider confidence. Through an understanding of materials available, new items can be planned and created. In an emergency situation, established practical skills are invaluable when improvising essentials.

Plastic bags can be crocheted into nets or rope, if you know how. There were reasons for all the different types of knots. A simple Iron Age style kiln can be constructed from garden clay for making pots, plates or cups. Clean drinking water can be distilled from muddy puddles using ordinary kitchen equipment. Scrap metal can become useful machinery – pulleys, crushers, presses.

Programmes about survival skills are popular entertainment. There are courses and holidays available where you can spend some time developing these abilities. It's better to learn under supervision. Wildlife, including many edible plants, may be protected in some areas. Unexploited wilderness, where natural resources are still abundant, has its own dangers for the lone inexperienced traveller.

Learning how to find water in a strange environment, and how to prepare it for safe drinking, is a crucial skill. Building a temporary shelter takes a lot of vegetation. Carry a light plastic sheet in your emergency pack to reduce this damage. Acquire a flint and steel, or fire bow, and understand how to source dry tinder.

A small but very sharp knife is a key tool in survival on the land. Master the art of keeping a good edge. If you need to skin an animal for food, you will appreciate it. Meat must be well cooked, against parasites, and there are several ways of doing this without utensils.

In the absence of meat, fungi are high in protein. Despite the dangers posed by mis-identification, they are a valuable food source. Most can be preserved by drying. Experience, preferably guided at first, is essential when harvesting fungi. Many have less edible, but very similar, alternatives growing close by. Only a few are lethal, though.

Our use of materials has radiated out from those we gathered as we migrated to almost anything the planet can produce. To become resilient, we need to look at returning to more local resources to provide the necessities of life. This will be a long process.

Practical Skills Resilience Plan

Not so many years ago, nobody was in the habit of recycling. There were no facilities available, all waste was wasted in landfills – ironically now being mined themselves for the rare minerals we used to casually chuck out.

Now, most people can identify at least four separate types of rubbish. Recycling has become a habit. It's easy to join in.

The same process needs to happen with the use of practical skills. It takes time to gain these. You need discipline to keep doing a little bit each day, persistence through the difficult parts and the ability to learn from mistakes.

The best way to learn is from skilled people. If there are none around, then become one yourself.

- Teach children to help with cooking from a young age. Make apple crumble, cut out biscuits, ice fairy cakes. Pizza is a good entry point for savouries!
- Even if you only have a tiny patch of productive garden, occasionally bringing food in direct from the plant is valuable education. Encourage children to take an interest in growing vegetables.
- Think about which other simple crafts you could use in your daily lifestyle. Learning to create with textiles and wood gives you clothes, utensils, furniture. Acquire a basic competence in repair skills across the board. Find out what you are best at and develop it further.
- Sign up for a day course in a traditional craft, preferably outdoors. Take a picnic. Deal with the weather. Did you enjoy it? At the very least, you will learn something about yourself.
- Languages, music and art are valuable skills; develop their practical sides. Where does paint come from? How are musical instruments made? Visit the country and see the language come to life!
- Can you make jam?
- What basic practical knowledge would be useful in an emergency?

Chapter Seventeen

Crafts Using Local Materials

The use of practical skills connects you to your environment in a way that just buying everything you need without regard to its provenance does not. As you work on a piece of natural wood, you become aware of its structure. The way the grain runs, the meaning of its colours; these acquire a new significance.

Craftspeople shared this knowledge with other members of their communities. The relationship between tree and furniture was well understood. Sometimes developing branches were actually bent into corners and matured in the right shape. You would have to order such pieces well in advance!

As more people cultivate a craft and make the effort to spend money responsibly, opportunities will arise for the use of local materials. They need to be respected as valuable resources which have to be incorporated in community planning.

A willow bed or coppice wood can produce an annual harvest. This wood is thin but can be woven into many basic household articles. Whittling and turning create other small items, such as tent pegs. Straight sticks substitute for imported bamboo as garden stakes.

Larger trees take longer to mature. An area needs to be set aside for decades to harvest quality timber. This represents a significant investment. Established woodlands provide domestic firewood, charcoal, wild foods and foraging for pigs. Forest gardening techniques are developing which incorporate fruit trees and encourage edible plants. Where flooding is a problem, trees can hold far more water back than open countryside does.

Fruit and nut trees eventually become materials for the carpenter. Other food crops generate byproducts too, such as straw. Hemp and flax are particularly versatile crops, providing both edible, oil rich seeds and useful fibre. The fabrics which can be grown in this country are better both for the environment and the local economy. Use your consumer power to create a demand.

Bee hives are encouraged where food crops need pollinating. Beeswax provides candles, polish and bases for ointments. These can be scented with oils extracted from herbs. Lavender for oil is grown commercially in Britain.

Once you have found a craft which you enjoy, try combining it with other skills, exploring the use of materials. You could make a drop spindle from recycled materials, dye your wool with hedgerow or kitchen plants, build a simple frame loom from driftwood, string it with hemp twine and weave a set of place mats, perhaps backed with linen cut from a worn out table cloth.

Cards for special occasions are always popular. If there's no paper produced locally, you can make your own. It's quite messy, but fun. Decorate it with pressed flowers, cut out magazine pictures for collage effects, learn calligraphy. You can make ink from oak galls or candle soot. Do you know how to cut a quill pen from a large feather?

Lotions and creams use herbs for scent. Learn about cultivating these yourself. Try making your own essential oils from plants in your garden. Which ones are most productive? Can you grow enough? Is your neighbour interested in making space for more, to exchange for your soaps and bath salts?

Move away from competing over the quality of a finished product. Instead, use your craft to gain an in-depth understanding of the materials involved. Provide a story instead of shiny labels. Visit important places related to your particular skill, collect or recreate old tools of the trade. How could your hobby help to preserve traditional knowledge?

Discover the historical use of resources in your own area. Are these still available? If renewable materials, such as wood or fibre, were easy to produce, can this be done again? What special advantages does your area have to trade on? Is there a museum where this information is kept?

Before fossil fuels revolutionised transport, most materials were very locally sourced. Large loads required the use of expensive horse drawn carts. Where a particular stone was needed for decoration, for example, the cost of transport from the quarry often exceeded that of carving and installing it.

Finished products are more valuable than raw materials. In areas of local abundance, artisans specialised in certain skills and exported their work. In a region with clay soils, they would find it easy to make more pottery than they needed. Metal ores were crafted into ingots by people living as close to the mine as possible. Salt was produced at the sea side. Trade happened

Although clay and salt are still part of our environment, easily accessible ores are not. Few mines remain which are independent of the most advanced technology. Most of the metal used in Britain is imported, mainly as completed goods. The resilient community will have to look at recycling, rather than prospecting, for its metal supplies!

Study the resources available today in your county. What stone is found where you live? What types of soil are there? What does it grow best? Is there clay for ceramics? Is there waste which can be used in new products? Used glass is a resource best processed close to where it is created.

Urban development generates recyclates. Rural areas grow food, fibre crops and trees. Watercourses and coastal areas provide other opportunities, including the creation of electricity for machinery.

If you live in Somerset there is willow and alder wood. Sheep and cows are raised, providing leather and wool. Hemp was once a major crop, supplying sailing ships with rope and canvas. With modern processing techniques, much finer cloth can be made from hemp. It can also be turned into plastics and building materials.

Flax growing on the heavier clay soils will yield linseed oil seeds but often only poor quality fibres for linen. Peat is still dug, on an industrial scale. Finished workings are turned into wildlife areas. These are important reserves of fish, game birds, and survival foods such as reedmace.

The silver and lead deposits have been largely used up by earlier cultures. Centuries later, some areas of Somerset are too polluted from this mining for food to be grown. Sandstone and limestone are still quarried, though population pressure makes expansion difficult. Disused stone quarries are often dedicated nature reserves.

Somerset has an abundance of water, which powered a number of mills. Paper making prospered here, as it requires a convenient water source as well as energy.

The process of achieving anything like resilience in this Reskilling section will be a long one.

Globalisation conceals the vulnerability of our resource base. Home producers are unsupported, often actively discouraged. Huge, powerful corporations pursue their goals at the expense of local communities. Governments refuse to even discuss controls on expansionism.

Meanwhile, do what you can with what there is. Try to keep traditional skills alive through practice and be loyal to local craftspeople instead of chain stores.

Local Materials Resilience Plan

It can be quite difficult to reconnect with your locality when it comes to manufactured goods. Go to markets and craft events, talk to people, visit the libraries and museums.

Raw materials which could easily be sourced in your area may be imported from the other side of the world. Creating a market for them can revitalise old trades at home.

Hence the importance of research in this section. Study the **environment** and focus on what it will support best.

- Use your growing space to cultivate scented herbs for home-made bath products. Which do well?
- Gather some materials on a local walk – driftwood, stones, flowers – and explore their qualities by making a piece of art or a garden feature.
- Learn the history of your county, its resources, its products.
- Value items for their provenance, for the story which goes with them, rather than for a sleek appearance and colourful labels.
- How would your environment support your personal survival skills? What are the challenges around drinking water, weather conditions, shelter, food, medicine, fire, sanitation? Could a small industrial unit provide helpful tools and facilities in an emergency situation?
- Campaign for new housing developments to incorporate small business workshops within walking distance.

Chapter Eighteen

Rebuilding Local Businesses

Think before you buy anything, however small.

Could you find it made locally, or at least in your own country? Sold by an independent retailer in your neighbourhood or on-line? Have you ever paid attention to the businesses in your area which are still owned and run by the people who live there? How many are in your village, your High Street, within walking distance?

You could probably find a few dealing with the 'service industry' – hairdressers, cafes, corner shops – but independent manufacturers and non-food retailers are rare, where once they supplied everybody's needs. Local craftspeople used to provide quality goods made from the materials around them. They would spend the profits on food grown by neighbouring farmers and market gardeners.

Money was spent in the immediate area to such an extent that many towns issued their own currency. Private banknotes were common; money was closely linked to the resources it symbolised. Under the Bank Charter Act of 1844, however, this practice was phased out. The Bank of England gradually established a relentless monopoly on notes issued.

The process of industrialisation and the growth of cities had carried demands for ever increasing production from rural economies. The land became over exploited, yet there was still not enough. Unwilling to exercise any controls on expansion, governments turned to importing materials. Taxes and rents left people in poverty as money was drained from them to pay for these, and for the military power necessary to force other nations to sell cheap. Money itself became detached from reality.

There are vivid descriptions of the decline of local economies in the writings of Rob Hopkins, founder of the Transition movement which promotes a more resilient way of life. From the days when nearly everyone not directly employed in growing food was working at some kind of craft, we have arrived at a place where most people in this country can do neither. To achieve resilience, this must change.

From 'Transition in Action'
"Money pours into the area through wages, grants, pensions, funding, tourist revenues and so on. In our current economic model, most of it pours back out again, and its ability to make things happen in the area is lost. Each time we pay our energy bill that money leaves the area. Each time we shop in a supermarket 80% of that money leaves the area."

A survey in Fakenham found that the number of vacant shops rose by a third after the opening of an out of town supermarket. These can take up to 90% of the customer spending power for the whole area. Smaller town centre outlets do less damage. They account for just over half of total consumer spending in their vicinity, but may encourage High Street footfall.

In Saxmunden, East Suffolk, most of the food retailers in the surrounding market towns expected to go out of business when a new Tesco store opened. Including their suppliers, there was a predicted loss of over a thousand jobs.

These suppliers could not expect the supermarkets to pick up this business. The latter typically source less than 2% of their stock from within 30 miles. In contrast, the established retailers which they displace may obtain over 90% of their produce from this area.

Independent shops struggle to compete with the buying power, credit reserves and aggressive pricing tactics of supermarket chains. They cannot match the huge discounts offered as a new chain store moves in on an area. Complaints to the Office of Fair Trading are dismissed. We are expected to accept that normal commercial practice involves deliberately putting small family run businesses into liquidation.

This rate of loss is increasing. Supermarkets are expanding into other goods and services, taking the business from High Street chemists, Post Offices and white goods retailers, as well as food suppliers. Nationally, one in seven small shops are empty. The figure rises to a third in some areas. The pressure to turn these premises into housing may mean they are lost to local business forever.

Where these new inhabitants are going to work will, of course, be someone else's problem.

Supermarkets claim to provide 'choice'. All too often this ends up as nothing but the choice between different labels on the same thing. The choice to buy from small producers, to pick your own, to buy British goods – these choices are being stifled under the blanket of convenience.

While the authorities impose ever more costly restrictions on car use in towns, the supermarkets enjoy acres of free parking. Even if the High Street is within walking distance, their time limits ensure no-one can go there to spend money. Local authorities who dare to refuse planning demands from big stores are punished by expensive legal battles. Chain stores boast about the number of jobs they intend to provide, while busily developing automated checkouts run by machines.

Supermarkets formed and grew because people used them. They were a novelty in a time when we believed a Golden Age of technology was just beginning. They saved time which would otherwise have been spent struggling up narrow pavements in competition with the new-fangled articulated lorries, not yet banished to by-passes.

They will change and decline if you stop using them. Above all, a local business needs customers. There is no point yearning for employment closer to home when, given the choice, you are choosing to send all your money elsewhere. It will be a slow process to change buying habits, even as our dependence on outlets run by global corporations grew slowly.

Make the effort to buy local and rebuild your economy!

Imagine how many jobs could be created if everyone tried a little harder to target their buying power. If a product was made using local raw materials, the money would go round again. Real, understandable value could return to it.

With the pace of modern life, it is sometimes difficult to put the time into replacing everyday household items with locally made ones. Buying presents, however, is something which requires care. Everyone uses soap and socks, cups and bowls. These can all be bought at craft markets and events even if there are no permanent outlets nearby. The extra price can be justified since this is for a special occasion.

Supporting craftspeople ensures these skills are not lost. Creating a demand enables them to rent premises and employ staff. Their products become easier to access. As their business thrives, costs are spread over more sales and cheaper lines can be created. With customers, a struggling soap maker with an occasional stall could eventually run a small shop, or even a factory. The nearby lavender growers would then have a regular market for their oils, again spreading the costs of production over more sales and reducing their overall prices.

Some small towns have shown an unusual commitment to local shopping, notably Hebden Bridge and Glastonbury. Their High Streets thrive, with a good number of independent shops. The general needs of a family can be sourced from these, though attachment to brand names is not serviced.

If you can't afford to replace an item at an ethical price, consider having it repaired. Quality goods used to be designed for this, and a whole section of business thrived on the amount of times you could fix wicker chairs, leather shoes, quilts and suchlike. Your buying in to a throwaway culture has put all these people out of work.

It may be that modern technology can help solve this modern problem. Small independent craftspeople often cannot afford shop premises and staff, but can sell on the Internet. With a county wide portal for local goods enabling easy on-line shopping, they could perhaps gain a larger share of the market. As the number of people choosing to shop there increases, it would become commercially viable to advertise repair services as well.

Food, clothes and household goods are not the only necessities which should return to a more local economy. Energy costs represent a substantial fraction of the domestic budget. Currently, most energy is bought from one or other of the large corporations who have carved up the market between them. Community owned renewables would keep this money in the area, again providing jobs and opportunities.

People fortunate enough to have hydroelectric potential nearby, including tidal energy, can use this considerable power to run factories. The saving in costs could enable competitive pricing. Fair Trade and anti-pollution ethics would be satisfied. Building up sources of raw materials close by, these businesses would become resilient. As the international situation gets more uncertain, we should strive to bring manufacturing back home.

The interests of globalisation are not well served by such enterprises, however. Their success will be obstructed by unfair competition, by punitive taxations, by every dirty trick the corporations care to deploy. Only a dedicated customer base can help them prosper.

Local businesses need the support and protection of the communities which they serve.

Local Businesses Resilience Plan

Shop local, with independent and family run businesses. Bring the resources needed for resilience back home.

- Write a shopping list every week. Can you order anything from a farm shop or box scheme? Many can be accessed on-line.
- Explore options for cleaning products.
- Buy cakes from a real baker's shop, or make your own.
- Cut the supermarket trip down to heavy, or specialist, items and go half as often.
- Find local goods for presents, stock up at craft events and markets.
- Plan ahead with larger purchases to explore reused or locally made products.
- Support the manufacturing base of your own country. Can you source white goods which are made there? Electronics?
- Can the loop be closed on recycling waste from your area into raw materials to be used in nearby factories?

Interlude Two

The Resilience Plan in the **Reskilling** quadrant is more about general direction than the specific actions suggested in **Resources**.

There's a lot of work to be done. Rediscovering the everyday skills taken for granted not so long ago will be a slow, steady process. Choose a craft to try out, and practise it for at least one hour every week. Give regular thought to the more complex suggestions. You may need to do some research.

Learn to view the things around you from a different perspective.

There is one action in this quadrant which everybody can do straight away. Stop playing the loyalty game with uncaring multinationals and direct your personal buying power at locally based businesses. Doing so will revive the creation of resources in the immediate area.

Even a tiny contribution leads to a surprising amount of money staying in the area to fund local enterprise.

There are about half a million people in Somerset. Imagine if, just once a year, half of those people bought an item on which a local supplier made a mere fifty pence profit. That would generate an amazing £125,000 for the local economy. Just that small effort supports several jobs and a workshop for the entire year. More jobs are created and there can be investment in local initiatives.

With a steady income from conscious consumerism, businesses can plan ahead. Think what you could create by buying local.

If small workshops are allowed to flourish, there may be enough business to keep an engineering firm going. The presence of factory machinery in an area means that it can be adapted in adverse circumstances to service suddenly more immediate needs.

It's important to support those able to take this forward. Recreate an **environment** where a range of respected craft apprenticeships are available to young people, not just careers as checkout operators.

Once everyone had a range of options to view while they grew up. Now you may need to start from the beginning, embarking on making things like a child. Allow yourself to play, to experiment without feeling like a failure. Don't give up, try something different.

The best way to learn is from other people. Being part of a group lets you access quick solutions, pick up good ideas, get feedback and encouragement.

And so we move from the **Reskilling** quadrant, where individual actions can still take you through, to the one thing you can't do alone. You are not on your own in this world, and there are many advantages in constructive association with the other people around you.

One person cannot be a **Community**.

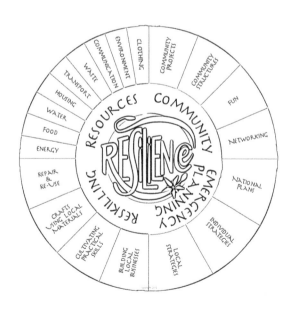

Chapter Nineteen

Introduction to Community

Who is your community?

Once it would have been your neighbours, the village, a small set of streets – people within walking distance. If you had links further afield, they would probably be family members, friends who had moved away, or business associates.

People used to spend far more time outside. They would be cultivating the same fields, walking the same lanes. Even when relocated into towns, most of the people in an area would be working in the same factory. Front doors opened straight onto the street, which was a centre of informal social activity. Children played, adults exchanged news, tradesmen plied their wares, and the occasional travelling show performed.

The sense of community is expressed in this description of Bethnal Green in London
"Bethnal Greeners are not lonely people; whenever they go for a walk in the street, for a drink in the pub, or for a row on the lake in Victoria Park, they know the faces in the crowd."
From 'Family and Kinship in East London', Young and Willmott 1962.

Individual houses in town centre terraces were often uncomfortably cramped. Retrofitting of the new 'mod cons', such as internal bathrooms, was difficult. The possibility of private car ownership had opened up. Many factors combined to drive the movement to the suburbs which began in earnest in the 1950s.

These new estates comprised low density housing, separated from neighbours by large gardens. Shops were concentrated in one place rather than scattered through the community in converted houses. They served a larger catchment area, so one was less likely to see familiar people. Car ownership rose dramatically. Crossing the road became a major hazard for children, which limited their freedom to roam.

The streets became the province of cars. Social life slowly retreated into the back gardens and fences between neighbours grew steadily higher. People today find it hard to meet others in their own geographical community. They use modern communication and transport to cultivate friends elsewhere.

Today, instead of expecting your neighbours to be friendly and involved, people will settle for an absence of aggression.

These people, and many others, relate more to a community of interest than a geographical one. A community of place has the surrounding area as a common factor, while a community of interest is centred around a certain subject or passion. Its members discuss issues and attend gatherings on this topic, but may know little of each other outside this.

These are popular, providing entertainment, enhancing skills through exchange of information, sharing enthusiasm, finding enough people for team games or a themed social outing. They are often dependent on modern technology to communicate effectively.

Other types of community are recognised:-
- A community of action is united by possibility of achievement, such as a design team. Idiosyncratic language terms evolve, there is the benefit of mutual learning and a loose informal structure.
- A community of circumstance is driven by factors other than shared interests. Sufferers from chronic illness, accident victims, prisoners or passengers are united by common circumstance.
- A community of inquiry relates to philosophers engaged in studying particular issues as a group. This was a new paradigm in that it recognised a subjective and socially influenced nature of knowledge rather than the Cartesian concept of objective unchanging reality.
- A community of practice is formed of people who share a craft or profession. This can evolve in a factory lunch room or around the office water cooler. Alternately, it can be created to advance this skill, when it may be linked to professional development. People within it can be geographically close, or at a distance.
- A community of position is more personal. It is built around various life stages, when one builds relationships with others at the same phase, such as the 'school gate crowd'.
- A community of purpose comes together for a specific limited purpose or during a process,

such as organising an event or using reviews to help you choose an on-line purchase. Members provide mutual assistance around this particular objective.

All these types of community can be empowering to the individual. They have similar issues with internal dynamics to deal with such as boundaries, clarity of communication and definition of goals.
Most people will have experience of at least one of these.

A resilient community able to respond in a coherent way to an emergency must be formed from people in the same location.

Using modern technology, we call our friends on the phone, send emails or interact through social media, perhaps meeting up for a night out or other special occasion. With the people who live close by, who we see every day, we can have very few dealings at all.

Who are your neighbours?

The people you share a wall or fence with, those above and below you in a flat are definitely your neighbours and you should at least find out their names. Remember you have the right to set personal boundaries and be polite in explaining these. You don't have to let the friendly lady upstairs smoke in your house when she calls, nor are you obliged to provide a taxi service.

It might be pleasant to play cards and chat every so often though, or walk your dogs together.

Our friends tend to be similar while our neighbours come from different cultures and life stages. Neighbours are diverse and give us a window into many different worlds. They are next door and can be physically there for us in a way that friends sometimes can't. Our neighbours expect little of us. A small act of kindness surprises – and you could make a friend for life.

Looking further afield, numbers of people are more important than area. Consider the work involved in leafleting each house, how large a hall you would need for meetings if most people turned up, any common issues such as car parking or flooding.

A good number for a small, but fully inclusive, community group is between one and two hundred people – a village, a few streets, a large block of flats. Communication is the first step.

If there is a local shop, you can chat to people and put up posters inviting interest in forming a community association. A notice board, on-line forum or an article in the local paper are other possible ways of generating interest. You should be prepared to become the initial contact person.

Try and enlist a few people who will help you with the idea, then organise leaflets and a meeting place to discuss it. Unless there is a serious issue to be dealt with, suggest a couple of ideas for improving your shared environment that could be easily achieved by a group working together.

Established community groups can access funding for projects, reduce everyone's living costs by initiating food co-operatives and communal vegetable gardens and represent the interests of the area to outside bodies more effectively. Above all, though, they should be fun to be involved with!

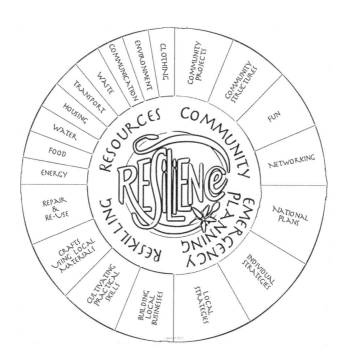

Chapter Twenty

Community Projects

Many of the recognised community types thrive without much, if any, face to face contact. A resilient community depends on this. Resilience must work without any modern communication technology.

An organised group whose aim is to safeguard a small area in the event of an emergency must be locally based and its members be able to reach each other on foot. The aim is to define the area covered, devise a series of plans for various events and disseminate the necessary information around the whole community concerned.

Once that is achieved, a few meetings every year may be enough. New people should be introduced, updates on procedure and changes in the area discussed. Until there is an actual emergency it will be hard to sustain a greater level of interest. Indeed, the people whose job it is to worry about these things would be delighted with even this minimum involvement.

It's not pleasant to think about emergencies. Everyone rather hopes it won't happen here and if it does someone else will deal with it. Unless one is upon you, it's not a comfortable topic for conversation between casual acquaintances.

The important thing is that people get to know each other. Any section of the Resilience Wheel will do to start this process, especially the **Fun** section!

A book club, a regular pub night, a walking group all contribute to community cohesion. Groups small enough to fit in someone's front room have no need to hire space and can keep costs low.

In order to keep an organisation active it's good to engage on projects. A book swap day, a weekend at a London show, hiring a minibus for an expedition to famous walking routes – these provide a break from routine. People apart from the regular members could be invited to join in.

Projects are also a good focus for starting a new group. It's better to choose a positive goal than to band together against issues. Many grant funding bodies do not approve of 'Residents' Associations' because these are now seen as too political. Call yourselves a Community Group.

The sort of project you choose depends on how many people are involved, their ambitions and the resources available. A litter pick requires a minimum of organising and improves the **environment**. A sewing club can make **clothes.** A hydroelectric plant could supply low cost **energy**.

Small Projects

Without funds to hire premises or pay staff, you have to depend on volunteer labour and the resources around you. What do you have?

A small scale DVD swap or garage sale is a good place to begin. Choose a location where people walk past, where possible. Due to the uncertain weather in Britain, it would be useful to have the option of a covered space available. Holding the main event outside will attract more interest though, so you'll need to hope for dry weather!

Charge a small amount per item. Provide tea and cakes to help cover the costs involved. Leaflets giving the date, time and place can be printed on a home computer. This ink is not waterproof so you'll need plastic pockets for outdoor display. There may need to be a trip to the tip afterwards to dispose of unsold items, especially if you are having the sale as part of a clear out.

If you publicise recycling and waste reduction in general as part of the event, it could develop into a community enterprise. Or you could raise funds to finance a community notice board. In order to become a focus for people to meet up, this type of micro event needs to become a regular, if infrequent, fixture. Every couple of months is a good interval.

There's a limit to the spare stuff that one household can generate, but a hundred can produce a lot more. It's a certainty that people in your area are going out and buying things that others are considering throwing away. If there was a regular swap or sale day to aim for, these could be linked up.

Even on this small scale, involvement with other people will need some basic rules. Is there storage space to collect used items? Should people just bring them on the day? At what time? Who disposes of left over goods? It isn't difficult to work these out. The important thing is to let people know in advance.

With more support, you could raise money to improve local facilities or fund an annual get-together. What would people like to do? Can your area become more resilient? Hi-vis jackets bought to do a litter pick of the area could come in handy in an emergency, if there was one.

Expand in association with an established organisation who can provide more customers. You'll need to profit share or grant them a concession such as the tea and cakes, but they can help you finance a move to larger premises. You may be able to find a local business which will collect certain recyclable items, paying your group a small amount per kilo.

With a larger event, you could provide some small activity for children to do, such as decorating cards or creating rubbish monsters. Make sure people know this is not a creche, as that would require various qualifications and insurances.

How a micro project develops within a community depends on who is there. A simple local sale could remain as an occasional meeting with tea, picking up some useful stuff. Or it could grow into a full scale recycling business. It depends on the opportunities available.

Exchanging second hand goods is part of the **waste and recycling** section of the Resilience Wheel. Other sections also inspire small projects with the potential to grow. If you're good at fixing bikes, arrange a bike maintenance day. Do it through the local school to involve whole families.

Are there a lot of people in your street driving to the same place for work or school? Enough to make it worth hiring a minibus firm for **transport**? Is there derelict ground or room for container plants nearby? Neglected gardens? Set up a growing project to provide **food**. Bring in non-gardeners by setting up a food co-op.

Running a small project gives you the experience to consider more ambitious goals.

Can your area support a corner shop? A household business spinning wool or repairing kitchen items? A small factory devoted to recycling glass? A renewable energy system owned by a local collective providing all the members with both free electricity and a substantial share dividend every year generated by profit on sales to the National Grid?

Larger projects

These can be spun off from the exchange of ideas in small groups, or be conceived as a plan and have a structure form around them as required. The primary movers need to identify the area affected by the project and begin to communicate with everyone.

Organise some inclusive activities, depending on the available funds and resources. A public meeting is important. You will need funds for a venue. If there isn't one nearby, this could be a barrier in recruiting enough people.

Larger projects can be achieved more easily by working with other groups. Your area may not have a meeting place, unused land or a shop, but the next village or set of streets may have. Invite each other to your fetes, explain your ideas and see if you can enlist them.

The meetings about the project need to be publicised. They must be inclusive so word of mouth is not enough, though important to arouse interest. Use the Internet. Leaflets and posters are cheap. Make sure they are at strategic locations.

Ask the local paper if they will include it in 'What's On'. They might publish a small piece about your project, or you could write to their Letters page. The local radio station may help in a similar way. There is always paid advertising if there is a budget, and social media can get word around.

Some projects, such as a Portacabin shop, involve everyone. People must be prepared to support them; to become customers, to volunteer or to agree to pay staff.

Having a collection to fund the hall hire at your public meeting is a good way of assessing interest. If this is disappointing, you may have to retreat to a smaller scale and build up gradually. Grant funding could support a pilot scheme to promote the project.

Other plans, such as a community power scheme, are more commercial. Not all the people in the area will be actively involved, but still need to be consulted. If you are consulting on a business venture, you must expect to pay the associated costs, so factor that in to your budget. If you are hoping to secure grant funding or investment, keep records of your community involvement history. It could also be useful for planning applications.

A large project, such as a water wheel, provides for the main people who have invested in it and who carry out the daily operations. The area as a whole could benefit by having an off-grid hub for emergency power. Community approval rather than involvement is sought here.

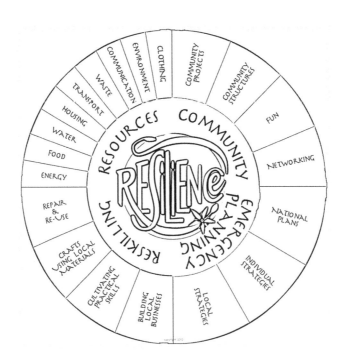

Chapter Twenty One

Community Structures

Once you are dealing with money, funding applications, takings or expenses, an official group should be formed. Having a structure gives you established ground rules to work with, clarity about roles and the expected extent of involvement, access to outside bodies for advice and continuity of the group as a whole.

There are different types of structures available. The form your group chooses will depend on its aims and ambitions as well as the resources available. Find out as much as you can in advance so that you can make the most of any free professional advice by asking the right questions. Do you plan to buy land or other assets? Do you expect your main income to be from trading or funding?

An unincorporated association is the most basic. Where the main purpose is public benefit and the group's gross yearly income is under £5000, you can form a small charitable organisation quite simply. The tax service will give you a reference number and you may qualify for Gift Aid. Currently, there is no need to submit a tax return for such groups.

There are umbrella groups for small voluntary organisations, which can help with criminal record checks, insurance or health and safety advice. They often have paid staff, whereas smaller groups will not. It is good policy to pay the expenses of volunteers. There are some rules around this. Keep in mind that your activities are limited to what people can achieve in their spare time.

If the turnover exceeds £5000, you will need to apply to the Charities Commission to become a charity. Their website is not encouraging. If you cannot satisfy their demands, there are other strategies available. An increase in income will probably be associated with extra work or more members. The group could divide into two smaller co-operating entities, both remaining under the paperwork radar.

If it is appropriate to develop your enterprise as a commercial venture, while still benefiting the community, you could form a Community Interest Company. This is a type of limited company.

You need to register it at Companies House. Annual accounts and returns must be provided, along with a community interest report. Corporation tax will apply to profits.

Directors can be paid for their role while trustees cannot. There is no restriction on any voluntary work that either can do. Both can be given paid employment by the group to do other tasks, though this is more difficult for a Trustee. Shareholders may be involved in a CIC, though if you are hoping to draw on grant funding, it is better to limit the company by guarantee instead.

One thing a CIC has, which an ordinary limited company does not, is an asset lock. Should the company cease trading, any public assets it holds must be transferred to another group with a view to continuing public benefit. This reserve group must be named in the Articles of Association at the founding of the CIC.

There are other types of organisations, such as co-operatives or partnerships. There is advice on the Internet about legal structures, business plans and funding. Much of this information is useful for smaller plans and different endeavours. It may inspire your group to be more ambitious!

No matter which structure you choose, there are a few things common to all of them.

Any organisation will have a governing body whose powers and responsibilities are fully described in its governing documents. This may be two or three people, or a larger committee. Within this group, it is customary to have three Officers; Chair, Treasurer and Secretary.

The Chair is generally the public face of the organisation, who represents it to other groups, attends official functions and may need to sign grant applications. In some structures, they act as arbitrators by having a casting vote at meetings. This must be written into the governing documents at the start.

The Treasurer keeps the books, records income and expenditure, issues invoices and receipts. With a small charitable organisation, these will be for internal use, but should be meticulously kept up to date in case grant providers wish to see them. In a more complex structure, there will be important deadlines to meet and certain accounting structures to use. You may have to find an accountant to help you with the tax return itself. There will need to be a budget for this.

The bank will ask for the governing documents before you can open an account in the name of the group. There are banks which specialise in community enterprises. A High Street arrangement can be made with them in order to use your nearest bank for cash transactions. A petty cash limit can be set, and other expenditure may need to be authorised by at least two people.

If the group needs to agree a large expense, three quotes should be sought and discussed at a meeting. Even if one is for no fee, but offers volunteer work, it should be compared to the usual cost in order to show its worth. Sometimes you can use the value of these voluntary contributions to secure match funding in cash for a project.

With funding, you will often find it hard to secure your everyday running costs. Many community organisations have to scavenge these from grants given for the latest new project which ticks the current fashionable boxes. Neither central nor local tax money seems to be available for genuine needs anymore, so you are competing against some very desperate people for a limited amount of cash.

The flexibility of a Community Interest Company may be a way forward. Encouraging the purchase of locally made produce brings money back into the economy of an area very quickly. A profitable CIC which funds premises with office space and staff can allow smaller charitable organisations to use these as a focus. This provides material for their own community interest report.

Finally, a Secretary deals with communication, including reports and deadlines. An agenda listing the topics to be covered has to be published before a meeting, notes taken during proceedings, and minutes circulated for approval at the next meeting before being filed and kept.

Minutes can be brief as long as important steps are recorded. If the meeting is noisy or rambling, call the group to order to confirm the decision just made. Technically, the record is often a draft of proceedings until approved at the next meeting, but it serves as a useful list of things to do and is generally circulated before then.

There will be correspondence to be dealt with, perhaps a website and social media platforms. Publicity needs to be arranged and funding bids written. The Secretary may be responsible for arranging meetings. Remember that a small group is a spare time activity and don't be afraid to delegate work to other volunteers.

There needs to be a fair way of selecting these officers, otherwise the group can become isolated from the community at large. Be careful of becoming too attached to a role, but expect the process to honour financial input and essential skills. If possible, each person should invest energy and resources slowly with a focus on results rather than gambling all on a major project succeeding. Community involvement from the start is crucial.

Some communities will respond with enthusiasm and things will go according to plan. If not, but you are still keen, remember three people can start an organisation capable of initiating micro projects and applying for grants to bring small benefits to the area. Perhaps showing people what you mean can persuade them to engage with it. The concept of privacy is important to people and attempts to involve one's neighbours in common endeavours must respect this.

Make sure your group achieves some practical results, however small, while planning and fund raising for larger projects. This sustains community interest during this long process, and provides a sense of achievement.

The grand dream of solar panels on every roof may have failed to materialise, but the resilience group has a thriving community garden. People can meet up there and discuss their energy issues informally. Eventually a plan may come together.

When forming the location based organisations needed to engage with resilience, progress can be slow. People may have very little in common at first. There may be nowhere to meet as a group. The area could be a new development with no appreciable history, populated by strangers.

Some people are just more adventurous than others, and can persist in such difficult situations. There are many networks across the country where these pioneering experiences can be shared with other community groups. Imaginative solutions, such as hiring a portable cabin to serve as a local shop, can be passed around.

A positive relationship with the people surrounding you is a major asset in an emergency situation. If you are accustomed to working together, so much the better.

Chapter Twenty Two

Networking

Networking is the exchange of information or services; to operate interactively. We are surrounded by networks. People communicate information at all levels from everyday gossip to serious matters with an agenda.

As an individual, you can join a network quite easily. Involvement in leisure activities has been shown to keep people healthier, and it is good to get into the habit. An established club is more resilient than an informal group in the face of people having to move away, or finding other interests.

If you have a hobby or skill, there are a variety of organisations you could join. Many areas have a thriving amateur dramatics group, a carnival club or a local football team. Most places have a branch of the Rotary Club or the Women's Institute nearby. These are national organisations and enjoy the benefits of a country wide network.

Although the Internet is not an effective substitute for meeting up with people, it can be useful to make contacts, especially if you have just arrived in an area. There are national forums for parents which list child friendly events, there are interest groups, and there are the major social media platforms to consult about local events.

If you are already involved with something, you could look at networking with other groups. Joint social occasions could be arranged, meetings to debate issues or exchange crafts. Representatives can be sent to regional or national gatherings, to share advice and experiences, find out the latest news or discuss fund raising techniques.

For example, there is the National Allotment Society for allotmenteers, the English Chess Federation for serious playing or the National Correspondence Chess Club for a lighter approach, the Amateur Theatre Network for actors or the National Association of Choirs for singers. Try social media sites to connect to fellow craftspeople internationally. Inspire events to support a national appeal, such as Red Cross Week.

Networking is not just for fun. It provides the crucial ties which bind a society into a coherent whole. Researchers found that job opportunities come via casual acquaintances more often than through close friends. Contacts in a foreign country can be very useful when planning a holiday there.

Experiments in the 1960s by Stanley Milgram and others led to the concept of 'six degrees of separation'. It appeared that everyone in the world could be connected in an average of six steps. This sounded incredible, but other studies supported it, and people began to study how such close links could exist.

Attempts at plotting these connections on a graph began to resemble the shape of other networks. Food webs, simple nervous systems and even the layout of the power distribution grid in North America seemed to have some fundamental features in common. The study of networks became important.

Linking people at random, though fairly effective, did not result in a 'small world' network. Strong and weak ties had to be factored in, reflecting the clustering of a natural community. Close groups of people have strong links. They are connected to other such groups through weak links, such as someone's aunt in New Zealand. These weak links act as social bridges.

Clustering provides resilience, while distant links are responsible for the small number of degrees of separation characteristic of small world networks. These structures are found where speed of communication is important, and it turns out that the Internet has taken on this shape too.

Further study here revealed another type of small world network.

A circular pattern most resembles everyday social interactions. Small groups of friends are connected to their neighbours in the circle and, through weak links, to other groups across the world. No single group dominates in terms of the number of links routed through them. Strong links, which take time to establish and maintain, prevail in this model.

In contrast, the Internet has a hierarchical structure. It still shows clustering and low degrees of separation, but is dominated by major hubs. These have so many links that most of the communication traffic is routed through them. Naturally, these will be weak links.

The strength of a hierarchy is in its ability to withstand random negative events. The Internet continues to function despite failures of individual routers. Undersea cables carrying the data for half a continent can be severed, as happened in 2012, and the network can reroute. It can lose up to 90% of its overall structure without fragmenting.

In an emergency, response is co-ordinated through a hierarchical structure. Authority relationships can be expressed in a way which is not appropriate in a circular network. This is helpful when dealing with sudden natural emergencies, such as earthquakes, where the existing community links will have been damaged.

Once the initial disruption is over, the community will begin to repair itself. Strong bonds reform and local solutions start to happen. It will be difficult for a hierarchical structure, formed of weak links, to continue. Defined by roles with no social depth, it is locked in position. Informed by distant leaders, it is resistant to adaptation. Dependent on key nodes, it is vulnerable to targeted attack.

At this point, it should either disband or withdraw. If you are planning to form a local resilience group, you need to keep this in mind. Although operating as part of a national response hierarchy will assist your community during an emergency, remaining in it afterwards can be counter-productive. Different people, communicating in other ways, will be needed to provide solutions for rebuilding.

Trust and co-operation are the hallmarks of strong links, while a hierarchy has to maintain its weak links through power and compliance. Strengthening the strong links within a community increases its resilience, and can build up 'social capital'.

There is much debate about how to define social capital, but it is generally agreed that it benefits the individuals involved. A strong community, or an 'old boys' network, may act to encourage or to oppress their neighbours. The structure is capable of both, but it should be noted that successful aggression will lead to the formation of hierarchical links which act against continuing social capital.

Usually, though, a strong community results in lower crime rates, more care for the elderly and increased prosperity. There are dangers here in becoming too isolated. Large scale events may threaten to overwhelm a single group on its own. Mobilising a collective enterprise depends on maintaining those weak links with other nearby groups.

It is not enough to peacefully co-exist; there needs to be communication. As this is only possible between equals, the welfare of one's neighbouring towns, districts and countries should be a concern to be watched and addressed where necessary.

One level upon which groups should definitely take a common interest is politics. A very important part of networking is attending your local council meetings. Public debates by ordinary people upon the issues of the day were commonplace before television and urban sprawl created their barriers.

In Britain, the date, time and place of all these meetings must be made public and will usually be on a website. They range from Parish or Town Councils where neighbourhood issues are dealt with, through District where planning affairs can be acted upon, to County Council where the major budget items for your area are decided.

Many councillors feel unsupported by the public when they are trying to promote local interests and would appreciate more people turning up to meetings. Politics is of vital concern to everyday life. If more people got involved, the whole process could be a lot more fun.

However, as things stand, council meetings are admittedly sometimes tedious and frustrating for the audience. Form a rota among your neighbours and take turns at bringing news back. Express your opinions by letters to the local paper if concerns were not addressed at the meeting, or if it was a particularly well conducted affair.

Independent councillors are at a disadvantage compared to those belonging to a party. There is a great deal of paperwork to read through and understand. If you belong to a political party, staff will do this work for you, translating it into their party line to inform your vote.

Much of this information is publicly accessible. If you want an effective local representative, you could look at supporting them with a reading group. Issues need to be debated within communities, not in distant party headquarters. Make use of modern technology to conduct live debates with input from community representatives across the country.

A resilient individual can survive. Within a community, they can thrive. If a local group is well embedded in a circular network spanning the entire world, its members can respond to distant opportunities. Remember that the six degrees of separation were discovered long before Internet technology became so universal.

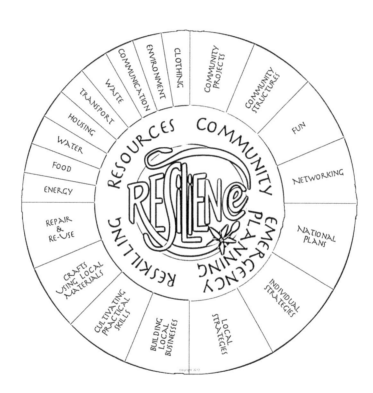

Chapter Twenty Three

Fun!

Find out what's going on in your neighbourhood. Someone is bound to have organised something and would appreciate your attendance.

Try a nature watching expedition. Some go out at night to observe owls and bats, for added excitement. See what banger racing is like, go to a nearby show. Explore a local walk in the country or around famous streets. A walk in green open spaces, especially if there is a lake or river there too, has been shown to improve one's mood and feelings of self-esteem.

Make it a custom to do something different with friends or family every fortnight. Having fun doesn't have to be expensive!

Revive the pre-television tradition of playing card or board games in the long winter evenings. Younger children can learn snap or pairing easily. Older ones can pick up more complex games. Set aside an hour after dinner for family time. The wonder of catch up TV means you won't miss anything.

Buy board games cheap at the boot sale and try them out. There are the classics such as backgammon, chess or ludo. New favourites include Uno, Risk and Stratego. Some games like Go, Mancala and Othello are surprisingly challenging given their simple materials.

The rules of most games can be found on-line, which is handy as they are often missing in second hand sets. If you enjoy a particular game, treat yourself to a new set. Better yet, make the board and pieces yourself as a craft project. Use your developing skill in constructing neat wooden boxes out of scrap materials. Sew a pretty bag for Scrabble pieces, or collage an old chocolate box to keep playing cards in.

The uncertainties of the British weather encourage fast-response fun. Seize the day by having a plan ready to swing into action. A garden barbecue can be organised quickly. Prepare a treasure hunt for the kids, using small wrapped sweets. A picnic doesn't even need a garden if there is a park nearby.

Co-ordinate this in advance ready for a good day. Keep in mind how people are going to get there. If there are cars or public transport available, you could venture out to a local beauty spot. Have a back up meeting place in case of sudden rain, or your first choice being too crowded. Make sure mobile phone numbers are up to date if several groups are meeting.

Someone needs to bring blankets to sit on, possibly with thin plastic to go underneath as the grass may still be damp. A wicker basket keeps supplies off the ground. Remember some lightweight, but not disposable, cups, plates and cutlery. Take travel wipes, and bring empty carrier bags to take your litter home in.

Avoid mayonnaise, tuna and other foods which go off quickly in the heat. Bring soft drinks, and water as well as it is useful for rinsing hands. A book, pack of cards, bubble mix or a frisbee can be handy, depending on the nature of your group. For the really ambitious, a fancy dress theme could be fun. Turn up as fairies, aliens, or characters from the latest popular costume drama!

Unless you live on the coast, a seaside trip will need an early start to beat the traffic. Add towels, swimming costumes, flipflops, hats and sunscreen to the picnic list and you're away! You could make yourself a Mancala set out of sand and pebbles at the beach to while away a sunny day with a tournament, as the children play in the sea. Try your hand at sand sculpture, or bring a sketch pad.

It's nice if someone keeps a scrapbook of your adventures as a family or group of friends. Postcards, some printed photos of everyone together or of sights that made you laugh, pressed flowers for decoration – after a few years, these will be appreciated for the memories they recall.

If you are new to a neighbourhood it can be hard to meet people, especially if you are working all day. Look for interest clubs that might suit you. There may be a book club, a sewing circle, a film society – if not, think about starting one. A film swap day could expand into holding regular trips to the theatre, especially helpful in rural areas with poor public transport where pooled resources can secure a minibus hire.

Adventures keep a group lively and interesting. Try projects such as putting on a dramatic production for the neighbourhood, organising a community day out or pub games night. Get involved with sporting events. An internet forum can help to communicate ideas around the area.

Holding a larger event accessible by the whole community is an excellent way to get everyone together and networking. It's fun, targets a specific aim, and is time limited so everyone is clear how much commitment they are making. Use the school field, hire a local hall or have the street closed for the day.

Street parties in quiet roads away from main transport links count as small events. Although there is currently no charge for a road closure order here, you will need to apply for one several months before your event. You may need public liability insurance, a risk assessment and signage of certain specified types. If you live in a quiet cul-de-sac, some councils may waive this requirement.

Alternatively, a large driveway, front garden or private parking area can be used for a get together. The more you involve your whole community in these, the longer they will continue to happen. Deal with issues of noise or drunkeness before they become a problem. Spend the first part of the day tidying up the neighbourhood and attending to neglected gardens to build up social capital.

The traditional village fete plan is a good one with its mixture of stalls, games and entertainment, even transplanted to an urban hall. As with extended family gatherings such as weddings, community events need to appeal to many different types. Include young families with small children by having day time activities, provide seating and even transport for the elderly. Keep music and alcohol in the background until later.

Invent competitions around both physical strength and creativity; tug of war, races, a fancy hat parade, guessing games to win sweets or a cake. Collect half a dozen hula hoops – does anyone do circus skills in your neighbourhood? There are many other ideas available on-line for games.

Remember to publicise your event and don't forget to decorate!

You can use an event for fundraising, or profiling a local cause. A small boot sale on the field helps to get people involved. A local radio station might like to join in, and of course there will be pictures on social media, even in the local paper! If your area is keen on sport, friendly matches could be arranged between communities.

Events run with other groups give access to more resources, and encourage networking. Work together for an Xmas party, a summer fete, or to observe a local tradition like May Day. This last would be especially appropriate for resilience groups!

The Resilience Plan for the Community Quadrant

How do you form a community? What happened to the ones we had?

The **Community** quadrant is less definable than the other three. Detailed plans depend much more on your situation. **Networking** runs through everything, and so should **Fun. Projects** merge with **Structures**, and progress needs to use all four at once.

- First, where is your starting point?
  Have you just moved to a new estate in an unknown area? Are you one of the elders remaining in the deserted village or terrace you grew up in? Do you live in a high rise, a mobile home, a commune? Are you about to begin work on your second community windmill?
- Define the boundaries of your nearest one hundred households.
  If there was a resilience association, these would be the people discussing food and equipment storage with each other. Remember that clear street or block names will help emergency services to connect with you. Be sensible; if there are only fifty houses in your village, that should be the size of your resilience group. If you're on a large estate with few obvious boundaries, you may have to involve over a hundred households. Try to keep as close to the suggested figure as possible, given your situation. It's designed to be manageable.
- Explore the area within walking distance
  There may be some small interest clubs going on. Unless there is a venue, a shop or community notice board, it will be hard to find out. Chat to people, but look further afield for advertising. Where's the nearest shop? The library, school, sports centre or religious building?
- Find out about inclusive community events
  It's hard work to organise an event for a whole community. Entertaining all tastes is tricky.

These events need to be supported as they are rare opportunities to meet up with everybody, from families to the elderly. As attendees, you have to get into the spirit of the occasion.

Going to the fete, the community days, the amateur theatre – these things matter. You won't see celebrities and you shouldn't get drunk, but you will be part of something. Encourage the organisers with attendance. The fragments of community left by the fossil fuel diaspora are often held together by a very few.

Consider getting involved. What could you offer?

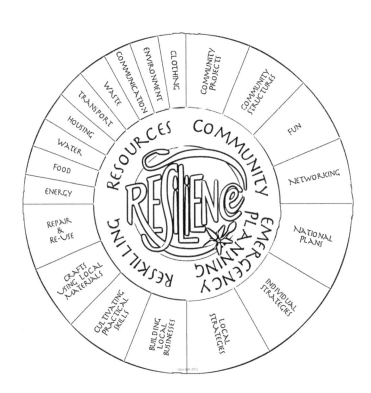

Interlude Three

The nature of your geographical community, its potential for involvement and the resources available are going to vary widely across the country. Your resilience plans need to begin with exploration and assessment.

Remember that these are the people who will be around you in a sudden emergency. If a resilience group forms, it will be here. You need to take an interest.

If you conserve water in your household, your next water bill will show less consumption. You will know within the year how effective your actions have been. If you knit a little each week, eventually you will finish that scarf.

Community is a far more nebulous concept than **Resources** or **Reskilling**. There are rules, but nobody says what they are. There is success or failure, but no standard to measure these by.

Self-interest has been encouraged for decades. People were exhorted to get themselves better homes, move to another area for a new job, buy more stuff. No weight or value has been given to community bonds, custom or tradition.

As these could not be defined in monetary terms, they were seen as worthless. The importance of social capital is only now being recognised. There is still a long way to go before these concepts join up. The individuals who profit from thoughtless development are not the same ones who deal with the social problems caused.

Learn your own strengths within a community. What can you actually achieve? How much commitment can you afford to give?

So now we turn to the firmly practical criteria of **Emergency planning**, where how resilient you are is measured in boxes of blankets and tins of food. Don't drift off into zombie apocalypse escape fantasies, but focus on real issues. What if you lost your phone? Have you backed up your contacts?

Making plans and trying them out is a useful exercise. Don't neglect details. Often minor mishaps can escalate into full blown problems. Pay extra attention when something has gone wrong, until routine is safely established again.

A resilient attitude can save your life.

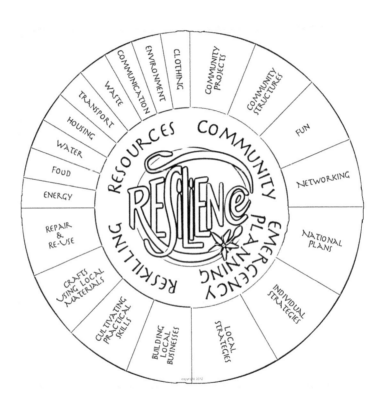

Chapter Twenty Four

Introduction to Emergency Planning

Most of this Handbook has been dealing with sustainable practices. The main difference between sustainability and resilience is that the latter takes into account unforeseen changes in circumstances.

Sustainable practices are important to create and maintain a stable lifestyle, which acts as a benchmark. Resilience enables the individual, group or species to return to this, or another, stable equilibrium with the minimum loss of capacity after a disturbance.

An unsustainable way of life will cease when key resources are depleted. Without resilience, adaptation to this change does not happen and extinction follows.

A useful definition of resilience is "The capacity of an individual, community or system to adapt in order to sustain an acceptable level of function, structure and identity" From 'Resilient Nation' by C Edwards 2009.

The ways in which this adaptability can be tested are many and varied. This section deals with sudden unexpected events and how you can be prepared to deal with them.

Suppose you were suddenly faced with an emergency. Would you know what to do?

Don't panic.

Look around quickly.

What has happened?
Is there continuing immediate and present danger? Has the water level stopped rising? Are surrounding buildings about to collapse? Is there danger from live electricity or leaking gas? Move to a safe place, using your judgement, and reassess the situation.

Who is involved?
Swiftly make an audit of human resources. Do they need help? Can they provide help? Summon assistance if you can, using the LIONEL protocol, which is just as useful on phones as with the radio communication it was designed for.

L – give the **location** in general terms so that response teams can start to head in your direction

I – what is the nature of the **incident**? What seems to have happened?

O – Are there any **other services** required? If you have called for an ambulance, should the police attend too?

N – What is the **number** of casualties? One, three, a dozen, many? A rough idea will do.

E – What is the **extent** of injuries? Can you see people who seem to be unconscious?

L – repeat the **location**, giving the full details this time, and ask for an estimated time of arrival.

Communicate this to the people around you. The emergency services may ask somebody to stay on the phone until they get there.

Begin to deal with the situation. Encourage people to move out of danger. Locate medically trained people if there are injuries. Establish an information point in a nearby safe place. Ask people to restrain themselves on mobile phones, sending brief texts to reassure relatives or change arrangements, not videos and long conversations.

Rescue of pets is best carried out as a team effort, especially if the emergency services are about to arrive. With more urgent rescues, it may be impossible to persuade people to wait, but they should leave crucial details with the information point first.

Each emergency situation is different. If you are involved with a motorway accident, there will be considerable danger from other traffic. A remote location may be hard for rescuers to find. Knowing some basic strategies avoids panic, allowing you to think clearly and act effectively.

Suppose your area is affected by flooding, although your home is not directly threatened.

Go out as little as possible and make every journey count. Your presence on the road is one more factor for the response services to take into account, so don't waste it. Bring in long life food, or start eating your emergency supplies. Try to avoid going out at all in heavy rain.

Driving at night is most dangerous. Keep at least half a tank of fuel, even for local journeys. Have waterproofs, wellies and a drink of water in your car. Make sure your mobile phone is charged. Take a map book; SatNav is only useful if you know where you're going. Diversions can be long in rural areas.

Driving through flood water is unwise. You can't see how deep it is, if the road has been washed away underneath, if there are any obstructions ahead. Don't change gears but drive slowly and steadily. It's best to be in second gear if possible. An uninterrupted, steady stream of exhaust gases helps prevent water coming up your exhaust pipe into the engine. Changing gear disturbs this protection. If your engine cuts out, it may have got water in it. Trying to restart it might destroy it.

Even six inches of fast moving water can sweep you off your feet, as well as concealing open manhole covers. Twelve inches can move your car. If you become trapped in a flood, call for help at once. Don't panic and think very carefully about your escape route.

Specific information is available on the Environment Agency's website. It includes guidance on preparing your home or business for flooding, including how to receive warnings from Floodline.

Fire is best prevented. Once it has started, there is little to do but run away. Plan an escape route should a fire break out at night. Fit and maintain smoke alarms on every floor. If you have to move through smoke, stay close to the floor where the air is cleaner.

If there is a fire - get out, stay out and call 999.

Remember - never re-enter your home until the Fire and Rescue Service has made it safe.

Take care when going to the window to look at a disturbance happening outside. Stand at the side so you can duck behind the wall. Hold something you can quickly raise to protect your face, like a book or tray, if the glass breaks.

If a bomb goes off outside your building, exit with caution in case there is a second bomb in the area. A gas explosion or earthquake can make the building unsafe. Use the stairs, not the lifts, to proceed to the ground floor. Restrain yourself on mobile phones to leave the airwaves clear for responders.

If you are trapped in debris, stay close to a wall. Tap on pipes if possible, so that rescuers can hear you. Do not use matches or lighters in case of gas leaks.

Many potential emergencies can be identified in advance and useful plans can be drawn up. Get to know your environment, its resources and people. Learn the basic concepts of risk assessment and combine these with common sense.

Care about health and safety can reduce the impact of adverse events. Maintaining electrical equipment, dealing with the build up of rubbish and taking care around hot oil are precautions against fire. Paying attention to sanitation protects against disease.

What possible hazards could affect your whole area? Are you at risk of flooding? Is there a large factory in the area which could release poisonous fumes in an accident?

There should be an official policy in place for these types of events, which you can access. Consider how you can engage with this. Could your community improve on it? It's often difficult to bridge the gap between emergency planning and ordinary life and get people interested.

A resilience group can provide a focus for this.

It's always easier to cope when you have nearby help, even in domestic problems. It's useful to have a neighbour you trust enough to hold a spare key for you. Your Facebook friends, and other communities of interest may not be much assistance here.

Getting to know people over a period of time is crucial in finding out who you can rely on when you really need to. People are all different. Some may be prepared to give a lot without expecting returns. Others may ignore all the things you have done for them when you need help.

An emergency situation is like an unexpected examination of your resilience skills. Do some practice tests. Put yourself in reasonably challenging circumstances from time to time. Go camping in a tent for a weekend. For the really ambitious, there are survival courses available. Join RAYNET or volunteer for a civil contingencies exercise.

The Resilience Wheel can be used as a check list to assess your progress. Do your plans cover all aspects of it? Will you have enough **resources**? Is there a **community** to work with? Can practical problems be solved by **reskilling**?

Planning ahead is a key feature of being prepared. Get to know your environment, its resources and people. Taking an interest in politics helps to influence decisions using local knowledge.

Don't allow emergency planning to be sidelined. It's not a resilient development if it hasn't got a viable strategy. Be prepared to follow the problem all the way to the top rather than allow your community to be put at risk.

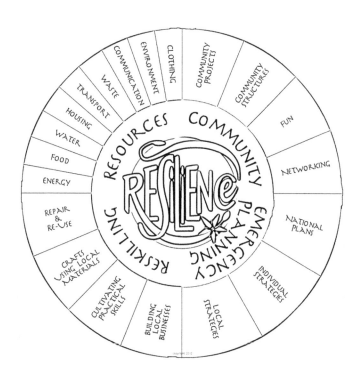

Chapter Twenty Five

Individual Strategies

What emergencies could affect you?

You could lock yourself out of your house, you could be snowed in for several days, or forced to leave your home for many weeks due to flooding. As the essence of an emergency is unexpectedness, it is hard to plan for, but there are certain basic strategies you can employ.

For a serious incident affecting a single household or small number of people, call 999 if there is a threat to life. In Britain, dialling 112 will also link you to the dedicated emergency line. Follow any advice you may receive, and stay out of unnecessary danger. Try to reassure others around you.

In the meantime, make a plan with the important information you may need.

You should know:-
- Where and how to turn off water, gas and electricity supplies to your house. You should do this if you need to be evacuated. Unplug appliances if you have time. If there has been flooding, seek advice before restoring the power or using the water.
- How your family will stay in contact in the event of an emergency. Write down their contact details and arrange a meeting place if you cannot get to your home - sometimes large areas may be temporarily unsafe. Make sure everyone can keep in touch.
- The emergency procedures at your children's school and at your workplace. Be aware of alternative routes between these and your home in case transport is disrupted. Know where the emergency exits are if you are visiting a building, and where you come out of them. Avoid lifts if you need to evacuate a building in an emergency.
- If any elderly or vulnerable neighbours might need your help.
- How to tune in to your local radio station. There is an agreement with radio and TV companies that if there is a major emergency they will interrupt programming to give public safety advice and information about the incident.

- How you will cope with your pets – have you a carry box for them? Is there someone to look after them if you can't? If you have to go to an emergency shelter, pets may not be allowed; can you arrange somewhere else to go?

You should have:-
- A grab bag of essential items ready packed which you may need if you have to evacuate your house at short notice.
- Some bottled water and ready-to-eat food supplies in case you have to stay in your home, or if the food transport network is disrupted.
- Back-up copies of electronic files stored in a safe place, and print-outs of the important documents (such as insurance details) which are stored on your computer. Keep copies at another location. Where possible, make arrangements so that you can work from home if required.

If you are affected by disruption due to an incident nearby:-
- Look for travel advice and work out alternative routes to get to your destination before you set off on a journey.
- If there is a major power cut, turn off electrical appliances that will automatically switch on when power is restored. If several restart at once, they may overload the system.
- If the water tap flows, check that it is not just fed by a tank which will soon be empty. Be aware of the route your supply takes so that you can find out whether it is secure. Make sure the plug in your bath fits, as you can store water here. Remember a full bath is a hazard for small children.
- A cordless phone depends on mains electricity. Keep an old style phone unit handy and plug it into the wall inlet if there is a power cut. Test this before you need it.
- The NHS portal has plans to clear its home page to provide information about what to do in a national emergency, as does the central government site. Bookmark these pages so you can find them fast.

There are two main options for residents affected by a disaster; leaving the area or staying put. Consider a personal plan for each.

Evacuation

Flooding, by river and sea, is the main cause of evacuation in Britain. Chemical fires in factories and farms can also affect a number of households at once. Gas leaks and even earthquakes could make your block unsafe.

You may be away overnight, for several days, or facing months of temporary accommodation. You may have to carry all your luggage; there may be transport available. Find out more about the emergency contingency plans in your area.

Meanwhile, your grab bag should contain:-
- copies of your contact list and other important information such as your insurance policy, passport, and any prescriptions you need. Keep these in a sealable waterproof plastic envelope.
- a change of clothes wrapped in plastic to stay dry, extra socks.
- Soap, a small bottle of disinfectant hand gel.
- a torch, a couple of candles, matches and a lighter
- a radio powered by batteries or a wind-up mechanism.
- any special essential items for yourself or members of your family such as glasses, hearing aids, nappies, baby formula.
- a small first aid kit.
- a notebook and pens.
- cards or dice are light weight and games will while away the long hours in the evacuation centre.
- remember to take your mobile phone with a charger, cash and credit cards. A money belt is useful; store this in your grab bag.

When you are told that it is safe to return home and reconnect your utilities, open windows to provide fresh air before turning on gas and water supplies. Assume flood water was contaminated by sewage or toxic chemicals. Wear gloves, and wash your hands before eating, drinking or smoking. Make sure all electrical circuits are fully dried out and checked by an electrical engineer before switching back on.

Using generators indoors to pump out water or provide heating can lead to a fatal build up of carbon monoxide gas.

You may want to prepare a smaller emergency bag to keep in your car, particularly if you are going on a long journey or driving in bad weather conditions. Take blankets, a flask or water bottle, some energy bars and a puzzle book in case you are stranded.

If you haven't been able to return home after 24 hours, there should be efforts made to improve your situation.

Isolation

A chemical fire could mean that people have to stay indoors for many hours. An area can become isolated from a crucial mains service, such as electricity or water, but not need to be evacuated. A major disaster affecting a key transport node could disrupt our fragile food delivery system.

Fortunately, in Britain, we do not get situations where people are completely cut off for very long periods without assistance being available. Again, weather is the main cause of physical isolation, as in floods or snow. Remote areas accustomed to this retain the decentralised features necessary for resilience.

Your 'at home' supplies can take this into account. You probably don't need six months supply of dried food, or a shed full of sandbags. A few weeks worth of tins, however, can tide you over unexpected financial difficulties. A few sandbags could protect your front door from a burst water main in the street.

- Calculate what you could get by on for a fortnight or so, in tinned and dried foods. Rotate these stores to keep them in date. You can take advantage of special offers to replenish them. Grow some fresh herbs, even in pots, to add Vitamin C to a diet of preserved foods.
- Have half a dozen 5 litre bottles of water. You'll need it for the dried food. The empty containers can be refilled from the nearest supply. Some purification tablets might come in handy.
- If you have the storage space, a caravan toilet - emptied and cleaned! - could be invaluable.

99% of the time, though, it won't be. Know where to empty them.

- Those few sandbags. You can buy versions which swell up in water, but are like small flat sacks when dry.
- Make sure you have a tin opener. **Never use a charcoal fuelled cooker or barbecue indoors**. Get a proper camping gas stove for emergencies.
- You'll have a first aid kit in your grab bag, but a larger one would be good for the house.
- Create that solar powered charging system described in Chapter Five!

Medical Isolation

This differs from other forms of isolation in that your mains services are likely to continue and other members of your community may be able to move around freely. The most common cause for this situation is a personal accident.

Suddenly you are stuck at home for some weeks with a broken leg, or other injury! Your stored food will come in very handy then. Have someone bring it to where you can access it easily. Make sure your doctor's surgery is aware of your predicament, and encourage them to arrange assistance where necessary.

You may have to self-quarantine due to contact with a contagious disease. People should not visit you, and you shouldn't go outside your property boundaries. Make sure you have a working telephone to call for help or supplies.

Use the old 'wheat stone' method to exchange goods and cash. Have a large open box, or marked area, by your garden gate or front door. People can deliver supplies and messages here. In the old days, a cup of vinegar was kept by the wheat stone. Money was dropped into this by the people in quarantine, to disinfect it. Modern technology gives you the option of paying for things on-line instead.

Stay at least two metres away from other people, and remain in quarantine till the doctor tells you it's safe to leave.

In a serious situation, an entire community may need to go into quarantine. The village of Eyam, in Derbyshire, protected their neighbours from the Black Death in 1665 by a particularly heroic act of isolation. The same principles apply as with self-quarantine. Government agencies may enforce this sort of quarantine, with a 'cordon sanitaire'. If so, not everyone in the affected area may have agreed to this, so community cohesion could be more difficult.

Finally, your community may decide to isolate themselves from the population at large, in order to remain healthy. This is called 'protective sequestration'.

If the situation becomes very serious, mains services may begin to fail as essential maintenance can't be done. Refer to other strategies in this Handbook for advice here. Remember the key purpose of the book is to provide a framework for more information. There is a great deal available on-line.

Protecting yourself against illness

The most important strategy you can employ here is to attend to your general health by eating good food, exercising and maintaining a positive attitude. Study various meditation and mindfulness techniques which can reduce stress. There are foods which boost your immune system. Do some research; add these to your diet and to your emergency supplies.

If you feel you ought to wear a face-mask outside, you need to follow this up by washing your hands thoroughly with soap when you get home. Make a good lather. Rub it in well for half a minute, then rinse off into an empty sink.

Face-masks are of limited use, but still valuable. They prevent you touching your nose and mouth while in busy places, a common way of catching germs. They're some protection against being sneezed or coughed on, and protect others against your sneezes and coughs. Dispose of them as soon as you get home, in a plastic bag which you put in your outside bin. Then wash your hands and wipe down door handles with disinfectant.

When using disinfectants, refer to the advice in Chapter Seven about combining different types.

Never mix bleach, or other products containing chlorine, with anything but pure water. If you mix these with acids (like vinegar), or ammonia (as found in many other cleaning products) a very toxic gas is given off.

Touching your eyes while out and about is another way for pathogens to enter your system. You may wish to wear safety glasses as well to discourage this habit. However, if the situation is that bad, you should consider staying in.

Travelling in extreme weather

Again, the best strategy is to stay in. Check forecasts with a reputable source if the news predicts difficult conditions. Consider whether your journey is really necessary. If you're travelling to an event, contact the organisers and make sure it's going ahead. Do you need to go out for supplies, or could you last out on stores? Can you arrange a video call instead of a visit?

It's not always possible to avoid having to travel. You may already be a long way from home. Using a credit card responsibly allows you spare borrowing capacity. It might be better to book into a hotel for the night and continue your journey in daylight. The extreme weather event may have passed over by then.

The metrological services can predict storms with some accuracy these days, but they can move faster, or be more violent, than expected. If you're driving in high winds, try to use main roads, where there is less chance of falling branches. Look out for side gusts, especially on exposed parts of the road. Your vehicle can be blown off course, other traffic may be pushed into your path, or debris may fly across the road. Take care when overtaking, keep both hands on the wheel and concentrate at all times. You are not safe.

Storms are often accompanied by heavy rain. A wet road surface is slippery. Stay a good distance behind the car in front, and reduce your speed. Investing in good tyres with a deep tread helps protect you from aquaplaning. As explained in Chapter 24, you shouldn't attempt to drive through flood water. Even if it looks shallow, you can't see what's under the surface.

Hail can fall with such violence that it could break your side or rear car windows, which are not as strong as the windscreen. Try to pull over during a severe hailstorm, if it's safe to do so.

Fog can descend rapidly and unexpectedly. It's hard to gauge your speed when the sides of the road are obscured, so check your speedometer regularly. You should be driving slowly, and once more leaving yourself a lot of room. Keep headlights dipped, or they will just reflect off the fog bank. Only use your fog lights when you're having difficulty seeing the tail lights of a vehicle in front of you. Turn them off when visibility improves, as they are a distraction to other drivers.

In winter, both storms and fog can be accompanied by ice or snow. These create very dangerous driving conditions. If you are caught out at night with a long way to go, you should definitely consider heading for a hotel or service area. A car park with facilities is going to be more comfortable than being trapped in a snowdrift.

Freezing weather may cause patches of black ice, and snow can quickly turn to ice on a road surface. Be very careful when using your brakes in such conditions. Stay alert for potential hazards so that you can reduce speed carefully. Sudden braking may cause you to skid. The advice here is to steer gently into a skid - if the rear of your car is moving to the right, steer to the right. Braking hard will make things worse.

Research techniques for driving on icy roads, and in other extreme weather conditions. You can even enrol on courses which teach these skills. If your work requires you to go out in bad weather, ask them to organise one. Taxi drivers, infrastructure maintenance staff and care workers could all benefit from this training.

Pedestrians can face many dangers as well. Apart from the hazards posed by drivers losing control of their vehicles, you are more vulnerable to wind-blown debris when on foot. Keep away from the sheltered side of high walls and trees where possible. If they fall, it will be in this direction.

You are unlikely to be out on foot while the storm is raging, but once the rain has stopped you might venture to walk the dog or go to the shops. Don't try to walk through flood water, especially if it's moving. Remember one cubic metre of water weighs a ton – as much as a small car – so a hand's depth can easily sweep you off your feet and carry you into the nearby river.

Go slowly on ice, and concentrate, to avoid falls. Don't turn your head to talk to companions, and stop walking if you need to consult your phone. Using a back-pack for shopping keeps your hands free for better balance. If you're walking in a remote or rural area during freezing conditions, it's a good idea to let someone know where you are going. Remember to tell them when you get back, or reach your destination.

Minor Emergencies

After all this drama, it should be quite easy to design some basic plans for everyday mishaps. The best way to cope with an unforeseen development is to relax your attachment to Plan A.

You're off on holiday with the kids and the car breaks down. Attend to safety first, which may involve sitting on the bank above the motorway in the rain. The hard shoulder isn't always a safe place to wait, though you should try to steer your car there. You will, if you've been paying attention, have a couple of blankets and a small sheet of plastic in your car.

Make the necessary phone calls, having made sure your phone is charged and has credit before you left. Get the flask and pass round the hot chocolate; open the tin of emergency biscuits.

Focus on problems in the order in which they can be dealt with. The problem with the car must be assessed. Until you know how this will work out, you can only put other plans on hold. Avoid wasting energy on anger; after all, the breakdown service may be able to fix the car at once. Calmly consider your options as you wait.

The goal here is to continue with your holiday plans in some form, preferably the original one. Some very basic preparations and a resilient attitude can turn domestic disasters into adventures!

Individual Strategies Resilience Plan

Consider some minor mishaps that could happen to you and prepare for them.
- Are your phone numbers backed up on paper? A small ring-binder makes a good address book, as you can add extra pages. You can even buy waterproof notepads and keep important numbers in your grab bag.
- Most people keep a lot of personal information in computers or phones. Using cloud storage protects this against your devices being lost, stolen or breaking down. It's probably best not to keep passwords in an electronic form, but figure out some other way of remembering them. Family photographs and important files can be put on a data stick, and a

copy left somewhere which isn't your house.

- Have you a strategy to cope with being locked out of your house?
- Find out how to turn your household utilities off, and how to safely restore services.
- Pack a grab bag. Can you lift it? You may have to carry it some distance! It's useful to have a small pack with real essentials just inside your main bag, in case you are evacuated by coach and are expected to put luggage in the boot.
- Do you have enough stored food and water?
- Consider how you'd manage if you had to stay in quarantine for a fortnight. How could you safely support neighbours who had to self-quarantine? What supplies might you need to maintain disease prevention strategies?
- Research the dangers of travelling in bad weather and how to cope with them.
- Start creating your personal emergency plan. Establish a notebook for useful contacts and helpful tips.

Remember to check the emergency numbers for foreign countries when planning a holiday. They're not all the same.

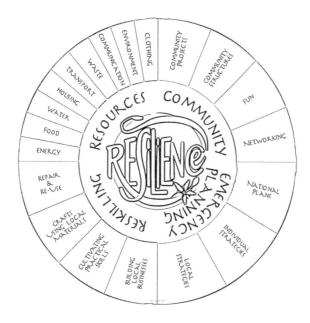

Chapter Twenty Six

Local Strategies

Community resilience is defined as "Communities and individuals harnessing local resources and expertise to help themselves in an emergency, in a way that complements the response of the emergency services." Civil Protection Lexicon (2010)

Communities should discuss what an emergency means to them and make appropriate preparations. In a rural area the welfare of animals may need to be taken into account. A resilient community needs people to consider these issues and share their plans with other areas.

The risks associated with large infrastructure may impact upon many neighbourhoods. Is there a major transport hub in your area? Are there bridges, key routes to cities, factories, power stations? Even in rural areas, stored oxy-acetylene and farm chemicals can be dangerous to nearby houses in a fire.

Any strategies must be embedded in the relevant environment and make extensive use of its knowledge and resources, not be run centrally and depend upon long distance communications. In an emergency, the travel and technology which have enabled most people to be part of communities of interest can be disrupted. Your geographical community will become the important one.

In a very serious situation, rural areas may need to manage without assistance for some weeks. Resources will be concentrated in the densely populated cities. In either environment, a community which has already paid attention to off-grid water and energy supplies, can grow enough fresh food to supplement rations, and presents a united front, has a better chance of recovery.

If you are forming a resilience group with the purpose of responding to an emergency, then keep to the limit of less than a couple of hundred people. Any more and two groups will need to form. Liaise closely, especially around shared risks.

Explore resources, study official policies, and form relationships with key workers. Organise exhibitions and workshops to stir up interest. Network for other resources like evacuation space, supplies or transport.

If you have to dig holes for waste disposal, you will need to know where underground pipes are located to avoid cutting through them. You should have established ways of receiving and distributing information, and links to neighbouring groups.

Making and discussing plans in advance allows you to consider more factors. A dash for the hills may leave your neighbour's heart pills behind. An organised retreat has spare medical supplies and ensures the safety of abandoned property. Can you arrange for the resilience team in a safe area to prepare an evacuation space?

Look at establishing a 'Community Emergency Group'. This will be larger than your neighbourhood association, but does not have to be a new group. Encourage existing organisations to consider how they might include resilience in their activities. Think about what might be required in an emergency, the resources already available, the needs and hazards identified, and how preparation could be improved.

Get in touch with local networks. How could you use their skills, resources and expertise? The Red Cross can provide free first aid training, the Air Ambulance advise on creating a safe emergency helicopter landing area, gardening clubs can work towards greater self sufficiency in the area.

Develop a Community Emergency Plan. Your local authority's **emergency planning** group may be able to assist you. It is important to involve them in it, as there will already be some guidelines, or even a very detailed scheme. There will be designated contact numbers; consider how and what you will communicate.

Suppose the responders cannot contact you in a crisis? The plan must include a way of deciding when to act, even without instruction. How much could you do with the skills and resources to hand?

Choose community emergency coordinators; people who are prepared to liaise with the statutory bodies who provide response services. Think about who would take this role in your community.

What might it involve? Rotating the position would spread the work load and ensure more people were trained in procedures.

Here is where you need a **community structure**. Decide how long this role should last – a year? More or less? A formal meeting to change the dedicated person should be held, with minutes kept. You will need to inform both your neighbours and the relevant authorities. Keep a list of the latter, and note any changes.

Key volunteers may need to take time off work in a crisis. A small group is in a better position to conduct detailed liaison with local businesses than huge national organisations are. You could enlist their support in other ways. They could bring supplies for a rest centre, or allow their premises to be used. Use your links to official policy holders to arrange these with correct procedures in advance of any need. Clear up issues such as insurance cover. Check at least once a year to make sure nothing has changed.

If there are volunteers trained and ready to mobilise, you could assist in an evacuation. Preparing people with door to door visits gives them time to pack and secure their home. With local knowledge, you can arrange appropriate assistance for the vulnerable. A strategy for pets and livestock should be in place.

Passing accurate information around is helpful. Post updates on a notice board, print out short leaflets, send emails round a pre-determined list. Keep these short and clear. Give website addresses or phone numbers where more details can be found. Add the time and date to each communication in an active situation. It may be over before some people return from work.

Resilience is about adaptation. Change your behaviour in response to the environment and avoid problems rather than having to cope with them. If you are not wasting energy dealing with situations which could have been prepared for, you can be of more help to the official responders. Although a resilience group needs to be prepared for the worst, a minor emergency is far more likely. Your street may suddenly be without mains water due to a fault. Heavy snow may confine the elderly to their homes.

If you have defined the particular group of houses which is your remit, having worked out its borders with adjacent areas, you can ensure that these hundred households receive suitable help. Supplies are often left at a central location and some people may need to have them delivered. It's quite hard work. Being able to limit this responsibility to a manageable size encourages involvement.

Emergency planning is extremely important, but it is difficult both to engage people with it and to sustain interest as month after month goes by with nothing dramatic going on. There is concern about the lack of training in civilians nominated as being responsible for implementing these plans.

This concern is mirrored in the dismay felt by residents as the authorities allow developments which will seriously impact on the resilience of their area. If every scrap of open ground is covered in housing, how can food be grown? Is there a hall big enough for an evacuation?

Comminication needs to improve from both sides. Emergency plans should not just be the concern of a handful of professionals, and the people affected should not allow themselves to be cast as helpless victims. A communication channel works in both directions.

Use your community structures to record advice sent up to policy makers. If it is ignored, make a fuss. Send leaflets round, write to the paper, hold meetings, stand for local election on the issue.

In order to safeguard your community you have to know what it needs. Not just in the good times, but as a reserve in case of trouble.

Bringing the awareness of resilience as a whole involves everyone. The other sectors of the Resilience Wheel provide extra interest and more immediate results. Emergency planning is on the agenda, but so is saving money by conserving energy and growing food.

By becoming more resilient in general, your community base will be capable of responding well to sudden adverse events. Remember, resilience is:-
"The ability of a system to withstand and recover from adversity." (Sir Michael Pitt in his review of the 2007 flooding in England and Wales)

Local Strategies Resilience Plan

First make sure that you are able to cope with problems yourself.

- Create strategies for maintaining **waste** disposal and sanitation, **water**, an **energy** supply and cooked **food** in your **house** in the event of a short disruption of mains services.
- Practise using water carefully, as if you had to collect it in containers instead of having it on tap. What could you still do? What would be much harder? How would you cope if the supply was cut off for several days? Do you know how to purify water for drinking?
- After these essentials, consider the roles of **transport** and **communication**.
- Could there be changes in your **environment** – might it become unsafe or damaged in places?
- Consider what resources you may need in an emergency affecting your nearest hundred households as described earlier, and where you would access these.
- Who may need help? Some people in this area could be temporarily vulnerable through illness. Visitors and tourists may be confused about procedure.
- What sort of risks might your community face? Are there plans for these at local government level?
- Explore your wider area, within a few miles, half a day's walk or a manageable cycle ride. What resources, skills and useful locations can you find? Could these be improved to increase local resilience?
- Is there a Community Emergency Group in your area? How could a small community resilience group engage with it? What would be the advantages?

There is a template for a Community Emergency Plan which you should find at http://www.cabinetoffice.gov.uk/communityresilience.

Chapter Twenty Seven

National Plans

An emergency can be defined as

"An event or situation which threatens serious harm to human welfare in a place in the United Kingdom; the environment of a place in the United Kingdom; or the security of the United Kingdom or of a place in the United Kingdom."
Emergency Response and Recovery (2009)   London, Cabinet Office

Emergency plans exist in all areas of the UK. The police, fire and ambulance services have tried and tested plans for responding to incidents, from fires to explosions, whether they are at your home, your school or affecting transport networks. Equipment, vaccines and antibiotics are stored around the UK and are quickly available to doctors.

Exercises to test these plans are held regularly. These involve the emergency services and agencies responsible for recovery. They practise responses to a range of situations. If you would like to join in as a volunteer, try contacting your local council or Civil Contingencies Unit.

The Civil Contingencies Act (2004) and the regulations that support it were introduced to provide a framework for civil protection in the UK.

Part 1 covers local arrangements for civil protection, establishing roles and responsibilities for local responders, including the emergency services, local authorities and utilities companies.

Part 2 covers emergency powers, establishing a framework for the use of special legislative measures that might be necessary to deal with the effects of the most serious emergencies.

This Act focuses on assessment and preparation. Another volume of guidance, Emergency Response and Recovery, covers response and recovery management.

An outline of the sort of problems considered can be found in the National Risk Register. This is a report produced by the Cabinet Office. It includes coastal flooding, pandemic influenza, and severe space weather interfering with electronic communication. It is updated regularly as new risks such as volcanic eruptions and meteorite strikes are added.

The Civil Contingencies Act defines two types of responders.

Category One form the core response teams, and include :-
- Police forces
- Fire and rescue
- Emergency medical services, hospitals and doctors
- Local authorities
- the Coastguard
- the Environment Agency

Category Two responders are 'co-operating bodies' such as the Health and Safety Executive, and strategic health authorities. Various transport and utility companies are involved here as well. Their roles will vary, depending upon the incident, but they are part of the local resilience forum, so are liaising closely with Cat One personnel.

These forums are regular meetings of all responders within a particular police area. They discuss local plans and produce a Community Risk Register. Your resilience group can help by adding local knowledge. Is there a back road which regularly floods, yet may have been included as part of a possible diversion route? Could you identify a safe place for a rest centre? What type of support would you need to look after casualties at home, to free up hospital space?

Often a string of minor emergencies can be more disruptive than one severe event. A flood causes a diversion. An accident blocks the new route. A fire breaks out in a chemical store; appliances cannot reach it through the traffic chaos. Although you cannot attempt to control the fire, your resilience group can receive instructions and act to reduce panic. You will have already discussed the risk and have a plan.

Networking with the Local Resilience Forum is important to support a response. They should be made aware of any plans which you have drawn up, and kept updated of any changes. Keep a record of where you have sent copies of your plans. You are entitled, in return, to be told of any new developments in response strategies.

Employers have a responsibility for the safety and security of their staff. All businesses should have arrangements in place to deal with the impact of a major incident or disaster. Make sure you understand what you need to do in an emergency at work.

A procedure for determining when an emergency has occurred should be written into business continuity and major incident plans. This should enable the person who will make the judgement to be identified, and state how they will be advised and whom they must inform. The person will usually be a post-holder identified by their role or job title.

An integrated approach should involve the following activities:-
- anticipation
- assessment
- prevention
- preparation
- response
- recovery management

Care about health and safety can mitigate the impact of adverse events. The testing and maintenance of electrical equipment, dealing with the build up of rubbish, protection against arson; these all reduce the likelihood of fire.

Fire extinguisher training is essential. Establishing proper emergency exits with lighting helps people escape through smoke. Practising evacuation procedures is important. The main bulk of personnel must be allowed out first, followed by any with mobility issues. This sounds heartless, but if there should be panic, people will not be prepared to wait. Nor should they, as this could put more lives at risk.

Businesses using hazardous chemicals need to be especially aware of the dangers from these escaping into the environment. A safe assembly area following evacuation may have to be some distance away. A record of who has escaped is very important to the rescue services. They will have to take serious risks if they believe someone may be trapped, and be less than impressed if it turns out that the missing person had popped out for lunch.

In the absence of forward planning, people affected by a disaster form a community of circumstance; the weakest type of structure. They are held together only by a temporary shared experience. There are often few pre-existing social bonds. It's difficult for them to look after each other.

A hierarchical organisation enables quick decisions underpinned by known protocols. The official responders, the professionals who have access to resources and who keep in practise, will be needed in these situations. Some, such as an incident on a busy city street, will always affect a random group. Others could be planned for.

The Strategic National Framework on Community Resilience published in March 2011 set out the Government's contribution to enhancing and building individual, family and community resilience. The framework established a programme of work supporting communities and individuals to be more prepared.

The Government states that it will:
- remove the barriers which prevent participation such as concerns about liability and insurance.
- provide toolkits, templates and checklists to help with planning, and set up relevant web pages to communicate important information, such as revised legislation.
- listen to your feedback and study examples of good practice, making changes where relevant.
- provide ways to communicate with the national resilience community, in particular local emergency responders.
- obtain useful advice from national bodies, promote and share the guidance from involved organisations.

Communities may require further training and/or resources to increase the resilience of their local area to a wider range of potential incidents. If you need additional funding, there are many organisations, government departments and charities that can help.

For further information on the Community Resilience Programme, please contact https://www.gov.uk/guidance/resilience-in-society-infrastructure-communities-and-businesses or write to Community Resilience, Civil Contingencies Secretariat, 22 Whitehall, London, SW1A 2WH.

National Resilience Plans

- Research your home and community emergency plan. The British Red Cross, the Environment Agency, the Rural Community Councils and all Local Authorities can advise on this. Central Government provides advice through their web pages. There may be a town or parish emergency plan.
- Discover useful networks. Organisations such as 4x4 Response could be helpful in letting you know what groups may already be operating in your area.
- Explore the pathways which the mains services take to your area. Are there overhead cables? What are the various manhole covers for? How can you tell? Can you find out where underground pipes and cables run?
- Identify alternative travel routes to key locations. Might these be too obvious and get congested quickly?
- Map out your immediate neighbourhood in detail. This could become a **community project**. If you could draw the utility supply lines on it, that might prove very useful.
- Lobby for retaining and adding to the resilient features around you.
- Get involved with politics. Standing as an Independent will need the backing of a reading group to help you to go through the huge pile of documents you have to digest on various issues. Politicians who work within a party have paid staff to do this, but then they are instructed along party lines.
- Bring resilience on to the agenda. It should be ahead of profit and the self-interest of individual developers.

Conclusion

Resilience is a valuable quality to develop.

Greater awareness of your surroundings leads to better coping strategies across the board, not just in a crisis. Try a new activity, cultivate healthy habits. Colour in your life with adventures!

Set yourself targets. Do something new:-
- Write a letter to the local paper about an issue which concerns you
- Visit your local Repair Cafe
- Spend a long weekend on a canal barge
- Attend a council meeting
- Sign up for an evacuation exercise.

Go along to a local event. As well as having fun, you may come across someone who can help your progress.

Refer to Interlude Two. Spending a small amount of money on something made and sold locally, just once a year, would add up to half a dozen jobs in the area if everybody resolved to do this. How much more prosperity would be generated by doing this once a month, every week, for most of your shopping. That's what to aim for.

In supermarkets, some produce will come from your country, even from your local area. Start to buy it, even when it is not on offer. How close to home can you get with essentials? Go shopping on market day, look for local retailers on-line. Travel direct to a farm shop once a month, combine it with a nature walk, a picnic, a pub lunch.

Everyone can use their buying power to improve local resilience. It's important to the prosperity of an area. Key resources are kept close at hand where they are secure.

Know where things come from. Be suspicious of shiny labels, advertisements, the latest trend. Is more plastic really helping in a world where all pollution eventually comes home to roost?

Resolve to learn how to make something. Don't let your piece gather dust after the initial enthusiasm. Set yourself the task of doing at least an hour every week on it until it's finished. Be realistic about what you can achieve given the time and space at your disposal.

Bored?

Take a stroll around your neighbourhood. Find out where the buses go.

Fancy some retail therapy?

Shop for crochet hooks and wool rather than for more imported clothes you don't really need.

Use the **Resilience Wheel** to keep a record of your progress in uncharted territory, to build on your initial plan.   Practise resilience in small things.

Keep things moving forward every month. At the very least, set aside just one hour where you do nothing but think about resilience and plan a single small action to take in each section. The steady progress is what really counts. Be as ambitious as you like, but maintain those simple actions. It's not difficult once you get the hang of it.

Sooner or later you'll encounter barriers. You may run out of patio space for pot herbs. There's nowhere to store a bicycle safely. Put the blocked action into a holding pattern; that is, maintain your progress so far. Watch for an opportunity to move forward with it.

Your neighbour might offer you growing space. The Community Association could obtain funding for a bicycle shed.

Meanwhile, choose another action to develop from your list.

With a total of twenty sections in the Resilience Wheel, there is always something which can be done. No positive effort is wasted.

You aren't on your own here. The move towards resilience involves everybody.

Where are we now?

On the edge of change.

What do we want?

Resource security for ourselves and our families. A sense of purpose, of being valued. Good health. The beauty of Nature around us. Time to rest and contemplate, time to go out dancing.

Start paying attention.

We have the technology to relieve the drudgery of cultivating food. This can be scaled down. Members of a self-sufficient community do not have to spend their lives in back-breaking toil just to feed themselves. Bring along the washing machine, the vacuum cleaner, the computers, the phones! Your wind, solar or water power can easily keep these going. You may need to leave the dishwasher and electric carving knife behind, though.

New social and financial structures are being explored in some countries, which dispense with the burden of excess rents and taxes. These new systems belong to a people who are prepared to accept their power to guide change, who take responsibility.

In Britain, we are a long way from being resilient. We depend on a global economy for too many of our essentials. This makes us vulnerable to events over which we have no control. Instead of continuing further down this road, we must learn to value our own land as the source of our basic needs.

This won't happen overnight, nor all at once. We have to think about our resilience now, though, if we would like to see a comfortable progress. The more we conserve resources, build up our skills, strengthen our communities and prepare for emergencies, the longer we will have to make this change.

If we start now we have time. It'll take decades for a controlled descent, carrying everything we need. Habits and priorities must change. Forests have to be grown, communities recreated.

Cultivating resilience is like carving a statue from a block of marble. You can't hurry it.

Somewhere inside the stone is the vision.

Concentrate on it.

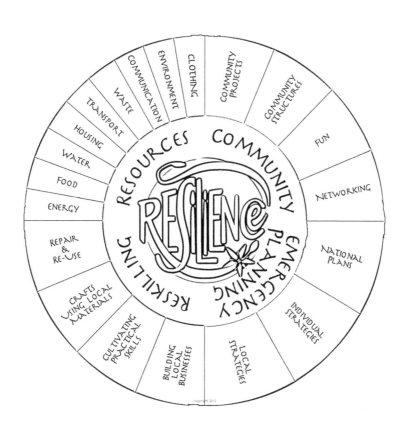

Appendix One

Your Personal Resilience Assessment

So you've read the Handbook and you want to become more resilient?

Ultimately, resilience is a state of mind, which is hard to assess. Fortunately, this state of mind is one which encourages you to take practical actions. These are easier to measure.

The Resilience Wheel provides a framework for you to discover where you are on the practical resilience scale and understand how you can improve on this.

There are twenty sections in the Resilience Wheel, arranged in four quadrants. These represent the factors which you cannot neglect when cultivating practical resilience. In this assessment, each scction has tcn questions, related to the suggested actions in the Handbook.

The questions are all about <u>you</u> and what you actually do. Not what you know you ought to do, but never get around to. You need to increase your resilience, and finding your base line is where it starts.

Are any of the actions already a habit with you? Have you been on the adventures, done the research, acquired the skills? Find out where the gaps in your knowledge are, and use this self-assessment to construct a Resilience Plan.

Rate yourself for each question, like this:-

- **0** = not done at all / never occurred to me to take an interest
- **1 to 4** = sometimes remember to do this / think about this / know a little bit about it / aware of the issue
- **5 to 8** = working on making a habit here / quite knowledgeable / have done this adventure!
- **9 or 10** = have a useful level of competence and feel that you've got about as far as it's possible to go here, for the time being.

Try the first section – Energy. Add together your scores out of ten. This total is your marks out of a hundred, so it's a percentage. Thinking about resilience in general, how are you progressing in this one section? Have you covered about a quarter of the actions? More?

If you prefer a visual record, copy one of the black and white Resilience Wheels, use it as a template, and colour in that fraction of the Energy section in the Resources quadrant.

Continue with the assessment until you have a final score, which you can also express as a percentage.

There are 200 questions in total. The maximum score is 2,000.

Add up your total score in all 20 sections. Divide this by 2,000, then multiply the result by 100. This will be your overall practical resilience level, expressed as a percentage of the ideal.

Use this assessment to work out your personal practical resilience plan.

For those who wish to know what their score means, the goal is to score at least 70% in each section, with an overall total of over 80%

You'll be pretty resilient then. You'll be able to eat well, keep a radio going – even a smart phone – and have enough water to drink in an emergency. You'll be connected to your neighbourhood and involved with decisions about it. You'll have something you made yourself. You'll be aware of any crisis plans which might affect you.

And you can prove it. Not just to yourself but to others.

National resilience begins with individual people, but it's stronger to form groups and work together. It's important that all the people in a group know the basics of resilience. Can the responders trust some random person to look after a hundred households? Of course not. You'd need to contact them well in advance, establish a relationship, demonstrate your competence. You need to trust each other too; working through this assessment together highlights the strengths and weaknesses in your group.

Increase your resilience bit by bit, taking small actions in each section. Some are easy to tick off, others will take longer. Establish new habits, become more aware of your surroundings, gain confidence in your abilities. Appendix Two outlines how you can organise your progress with a Resilience Plan.

Do the assessment again in a year, and compare it to the earlier one. How has your score improved? What should you work on next?

Good luck with the adventure!

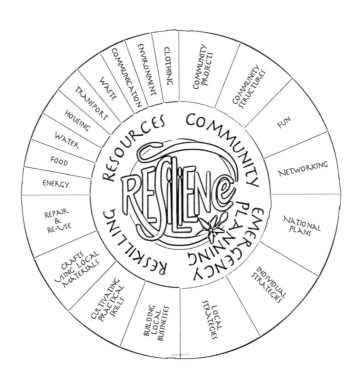

	Resources Quadrant - Energy	Score out of 10
1	Do you understand your energy bills and know how they relate to your heating and hot water?	
2	Have you used all the home insulating strategies you can, and know how you could improve on them?	
3	Do you always turn off lights and devices? If you are using a battery back-up system, these habits really matter. Learn to value electricity.	
4	Do you use rechargeable batteries for small gadgets?	
5	Are you aware of candle safety if you need to use these for emergency lighting?	
6	Do you have a plan to replace appliances as they wear out with lower energy options, including lifestyle changes. Research this for all your household equipment in advance, and know where to buy local.	
7	Do you understand small scale domestic renewables, 12 volt systems, and battery storage? Do you know how to use regulators and inverters in an emergency power supply? This knowledge empowers you to construct a system from scavenged materials.	
8	Can you calculate how much of your home could run on a supply of 2 kilowatts of electricity? This is the maximum output you're likely to get from a small generator, which must be run outside.	
9	Are you aware of how a house like yours could be designed to allow you to use more renewable energy? Visit an off-grid house, attend an event run on wind, solar or water power, go on a barge holiday.	
10	Have you researched community power schemes enough to have an informed opinion on developments? Could the people in your area benefit from such a scheme?	
	How much of this have you covered? Add up your total scores for each action. This will give you a percentage score for this section	

Any device which provides heating or light carries a risk of fire. The long detailed instructions which come with any electrical goods can be a useful source of general safety information. The resilient household will have a small fire extinguisher and know how to use it.

	Resources Quadrant - Food	Score out of 10
1	Do you cook from ingredients at least twice a week?	
2	Do you cut down on food waste by shopping with a list and planning ahead to use up leftovers?	
3	How are you doing with growing food? Do you grow herbs and salad leaves where you can? Could you cultivate a vegetable garden? Remember that you can score for having knowledge and experience, even if your present circumstances don't allow you to put this into practise.	
4	Do you shop for food in your high street or market? How much fresh produce could you get delivered from a local supplier?	
5	Do you know which foods contain important vitamins and minerals and how to work out a balanced diet?	
6	Do you maintain a store of tinned and dried foods for emergencies?	
7	Is there a food co-operative in your area? A neighbourhood buying group or community supported agriculture?	
8	re you cultivating your nearest available growing space? If you are already owing vegetables in your garden, you score here as well as in Q3!	
9	Are you confident with identifying edible wild plants? In an emergency, it's unlikely there will be enough of these to see you through. You can, however, practise selective weeding in your growing space to ensure these hardy edibles remain. Go on a guided foraging walk.	
10	Have you tried living on your 'default' meat and dairy for a week, as described in Chapter 6? As a reminder, this is roughly half a kilogram of meat per person. You can have two and a half litres of milk instead, or a combination of both. One litre of milk makes about 150 grams of cheese, or 30 grams of butter. You score 10 here if you actually did it without cheating!	
	For Q10, consider how much imported food – as in food which does not grow in this country - you ate that week. This includes all soya products, olive oil, most nuts, and avocados. Deduct one point for every 100 grams.	

	Resources Quadrant - Water	Score out of 10
1	Do you understand your water bills?	
2	Do you use all available measures to conserve water in your house?	
3	Do you collect rainwater and reuse grey water where possible?	
4	Do you use hand made soaps or other local products to wash your hair rather than commercial shampoos?	
5	Do you find, make and use cleaning products which cause minimum pollution?	
6	Do you keep your plumbing system in good repair? Does your bath plug fit properly, to create an emergency water store?	
7	Have you visited a reed bed system, a hydroelectric power station, a water treatment works? Your resilience plan needs to include outings like this. They provide valuable experience and are something of an adventure! Take pictures and talk about the visit on social media.	
8	Do you know how to make distilled water for drinking? Could you make and use a simple filtration system from scavenged materials? Would you still need to boil the water before drinking, or cooking with it?	
9	Have you ever explored canals or rivers on a holiday or day out? Another opportunity for adventure! Walking beside water is usually very relaxing. You may see some wildlife, especially if you go the whole way and hire a barge for the weekend.	
10	Do you know the location of your nearest well or spring? Could one be restored? Are there national organisations who might help with this?	
	How much of this have you covered? Add up your total scores for each action. This will give you a percentage score for this section	

	Resources Quadrant - Housing	Score out of 10
1	Is your home well insulated? Do you know about the types of materials available, and which can be used in retrofitting? Another opportunity to score twice for particularly resilient behaviour, as this was mentioned under Energy. A well-insulated home can be kept from freezing or damp with the smallest of heaters in an emergency.	
2	Do you use any outside space you have? Score again if you grow food there. Consider also that a washing line dries your clothes using free solar power, a small gathering of friends and neighbours helps community cohesion, and a secure shed keeps useful garden tools available.	
3	Do you care for your furniture and look for locally made or second hand replacements?	
4	Do you source the materials for do-it-yourself projects to benefit your local economy, and choose sustainable options?	
5	Do you know how to turn your mains services on and off? How to make your house safe and secure in case of an evacuation?	
6	Have you considered how you could manage without a fridge or freezer? Are your emergency supplies independent of mains power provision?	
7	Do you know how to make or repair a table, a rocking chair, an upholstered settee, a rug? Have you tried?	
8	Do you know how to provide essential services in your house during an interruption of mains supplies? What would you do if the water, gas or electricity went off? Would your plan see you through overnight – could you last for a few weeks?	
9	Do you remember to value garden and food storage space when looking for a different house? Take a day trip to a historical house to study their facilities.	
10	Have you thought about buying into a community eco-housing plan? Research the issues involved until you can discuss this possibility with confidence.	
	How much of this have you covered? Add up your total scores for each action. This will give you a percentage score for this section	

	Resources Quadrant - Transport	Score out of 10
1	Do you walk around your neighbourhood regularly?	
2	Do you use public transport at least once a month, even if you have a private car? Take a day out, or a weekend away, travelling by train or bus.	
3	Do you choose to buy food and goods with the lowest transport costs in terms of energy used? You may need to do some research here.	
4	Can you ride and maintain a bicycle?	
5	Do you drive for fuel economy and keep your car serviced for efficiency?	
6	Have you made a transport plan for yourself in case you cannot use your own car?	
7	Could you change to an electric or hybrid fuel car? If you haven't, have you identified the barriers to doing so?	
8	Do you know if there are there any car-sharing schemes near you? What about lift-sharing?	
9	Plan a holiday without flying, where the travel is part of the experience.	
10	How would you design a community transport hub for your area?	
	For questions 5, 6 and 7 – score yourself 10 if you don't have a car **A reminder of the scoring system:-** • **0** = not done at all / never occurred to me to take an interest • **1 to 4** = sometimes remember to do this / think about this / know a little bit about it / aware of the issue • **5 to 8** = working on making a habit here / quite knowledgeable / have done this adventure! • **9 or 10** = have a useful level of competence and feel that you've got about as far as it's possible to go here, for the time being.	

	Resources Quadrant - Waste and Recycling	Score out of 10
1	Do you take steps to reduce the amount of potential waste coming into your house?	
2	Can you have milk delivered in bottles? If you use non-dairy milks, are they imported? Is the packaging reusable?	
3	Do you avoid disposables and buy refillables? Pens are a good place to start. You'll need to learn to be careful with refillable pens, as they are more expensive. Bring more quality products into your lifestyle!	
4	Do you recycle everything that is collected in your area, and from all your household bins, not just the kitchen one? Do you rinse out food tins and plastic bottles for recycling?	
5	What do the recycling symbols on packaging mean?	
6	Do you know about the recycling process for different materials, and recycle things that aren't collected? Where's your nearest tip, and what happens to the rubbish from there?	
7	Could you buy things like cleaning products in bulk and transfer smaller amounts to your own re-usable containers?	
8	When buying new goods, do you look for ease of repair by a small local firm as a feature?	
9	Have you ever been on a guided tour of a modern recycling plant? This is the adventure for the section – score 10 when you've achieved it!	
10	Have you thought whether glass, paper or card can be collected and processed in your area by a locally owned firm? How could you support this?	
	Add up your total scores for each action. This will give you a percentage score for this section. **How many disposable products are there in your household? Which ones could you replace?**	

	Resources Quadrant - Communication	Score out of 10
1	Do you know where you could display information so that your neighbours will see it?	
2	Do you go to a pub, cafe or hall in your area where people who live nearby can meet up?	
3	Have you found the locally based on-line forums, Freecycle groups and Facebook pages?	
4	Do you belong to a club or group with a common interest? Join in on a day out; some expeditions are open to non-members.	
5	What knowledge and skills could you share? Have you thought about how to do this?	
6	How good are you at Morse code and semaphore?	
7	Do you keep an old style wall phone unit in case of power cuts? If you only use a mobile phone, have you a portable 'power bank', or small solar system to keep it charged?	
8	Do you have a plan for communicating with your family where mobile phone use is restricted?	
9	Can you create an emergency charging station suitable for phones, computers and radios?	
10	Have you got a portable FM radio? Do you practise finding the key radio stations used in an emergency?	
	Add up your total scores for each action. This will give you a percentage score for this section. **If you have to leave your home suddenly, it's useful to have somewhere to leave a brief note for family or friends. As with spare keys, this needs to be arranged in advance.**	

	Resources Quadrant - Clothing	Score out of 10
1	Do you make sure all your old clothing and fabric gets recycled?	
2	When buying clothes, do you seek alternatives to cotton and synthetic fibres?	
3	Can you carry out basic sewing tasks – buttons, patches, hems?	
4	How can you identify quality in clothes? Certain labels have a good reputation, but you can examine the seams, the way the zips are finished and other clues.	
5	Are you careful with your clothes when washing them?	
6	Are you in the habit of taking your outdoor shoes off when you come home?	
7	Do you know a local person who can make a good job of tricky repairs such as zips?	
8	What textile related groups there are in your area? A sewing circle, a clothes swap? Could they help you with Q7?	
9	Are you familiar with basic types of material and know which ones could be grown or processed in your area? Visit an appropriate farm or factory – perhaps with the group from Q8!	
10	Are you able to make a useful household item from wool, yarns or fabric? You can score for something that works, even if it doesn't look perfect!	
	Add up your total scores for each action. This will give you a percentage score for this section. **It's very important to acquire the habit of looking after clothes, then you can afford to invest in quality items which are locally made. These will be much more expensive than clothes that have come from the other side of the world.** **Consider why this is the case.**	

	Resources Quadrant - Environment	Score out of 10
1	Do you consider the welfare of wildlife in your area?	
2	If you have a garden, do you avoid the use of chemicals?	
3	Visit an organic farm, a forest garden, or a permaculture grower. Compare these to the environments associated with industrial agriculture.	
4	Have you ever planted a nut tree, or other food tree? Community groups often have tree-planting days going on; join in.	
5	Do you take an interest in development around you and lobby for more sustainable features?	
6	What do you know about your local environment, its history and the way resources have been used?	
7	Always ask questions. How much food does a conventional farm produce compared with the organic alternatives?	
8	Where does money come from? Where does it go?	
9	How does a debt based economy work, and what are the alternatives?	
10	Could you design a 200 year plan to reduce the population of the British Isles to its carrying capacity, while retaining an acceptable quality of life for everyone? What are the alternatives?	
	Add up your total scores for each action. This will give you a percentage score for this section. **You've now scored yourself out of 10 in nine sections of the Resilience Wheel. The maximum score is 90. Divide your total for the Resources quadrant by 90 and multiply by 100 to get your percentage score so far.** **For example, if your overall score was 36, your percentage would be 40%**	

Reskilling

Making and repairing the things you need has fallen into serious decline. Once local materials would be grown; now they are just as likely to be discards from some manufacturing process. Traditional skills are being lost, and local businesses declining.

There's a lot to do in this quadrant. Your options depend on a number of factors. Which crafts are you attracted to? Which ones are practical, given your personal resources?

It's important to acquire and establish a new set of priorities. Plan what to do the next time something breaks. Think about how things are made. How would it help your practical resilience if more resources were available in your area?

Household goods don't break on demand, and you may not need to buy anything right now. Your assessment here should be based on how much control you feel you have over the stuff in your life, but you do have to have done some real actions to test this. It's important to be able to quote your experience, what actually happened when you did this.

Access to locally based production and repair services can be difficult, and reducing the barriers may need help from the Community quadrant.

Two actions are of key importance here, and you should aim to do them every week.

Choose a craft to learn, and practise it for an hour.

You have to learn how it feels to make something by hand to appreciate its value, and understand the price being asked. Something simple, like crochet or knitting, will do. Try making a game board, with pieces. Or go for something more ambitious.

Buy something from an independent local trader.

These retail outlets, whether small shops or market stalls, are more likely to buy locally produced items than are chain stores where stock is handled through a remote head office. You have to support their existence.

Score yourself as before:-

- **0** = not done at all / never occurred to me to take an interest
- **1 to 4** = sometimes remember to do this / think about this / know a little bit about it / aware of the issue
- **5 to 8** = working on making a habit here / quite knowledgeable / have done this adventure!
- **9 or 10** = have a useful level of competence and feel that you've got about as far as it's possible to go here, for the time being.

Note some actions you could plan to take, or improve on.

	Reskilling Quadrant – Repair and Re-use	Score out of 10
1	Choose an important household item and start to research. Are you buying quality goods which can be repaired? How can you tell?	
2	Explore Freecycle and look for other places on-line where you can access local exchanges. Plan even small purchases, and look for things you need at boot sales. You can save a lot of money doing this.	
3	Find a holiday destination with a Repair Cafe nearby. Check opening times on-line – some are only held once a month – and visit for a cup of tea.	
4	How many basic repairs around your house can you do?	
5	What sort of tools do you own? Could you improve your tool kit to enable you to do more repairs? Take a look at the sorts of glues and fillers available; do you know which ones are appropriate for particular tasks? Do you make a note of any paint colours you've used so you can touch up a repair?	
6	Take a good look at the things around you and learn more about where they came from, how they were made.	
7	Is there a local repair service for electrical and gas appliances? You need accredited technicians for this. Note which brand names they can deal with.	
8	Pursue quality in more detail – read on-line reviews, ask opinions. An item which is well-made, easily repairable and ethically sourced will usually be more expensive when new than a piece of disposable rubbish with built-in obsolescence. What second-hand options are accessible for you? Does an item like this have a good resale value? Would its extra lifespan cover the extra cost?	
9	Do you make a habit of researching your purchases, large or small?	
10	Do you always look for the local option before spending money? Refer to Interlude Two for a reminder of how important this is in supporting your local economy.	
	Add up your total scores for each action. This will give you a percentage score for this section.	

	Reskilling Quadrant – Practical Skills	Score out of 10
1	Can you cook from ingredients? Do you do this regularly?	
2	Can you grow vegetables? Do you know how to use, and look after, gardening tools?	
3	Do you know how to identify clean drinking water, how to filter and process water which might be unsafe?	
4	Have you a basic competence in general repair skills? Do you have a reasonably comprehensive tool kit and know how to care for these?	
5	Can you make jam? You have to have done this to score. Pickles, chutneys or syrups count, if you don't like jam, but they have to be still edible after several months.	
6	Have you considered what basic practical knowledge could be useful in an emergency?	
7	Think about which crafts might be useful in your daily lifestyle, do some research and try things out	
8	Sign up for a day course in a traditional craft, preferably outdoors. Build a holiday around this if you like. Travel by train, stay in a family run guest house, take a few days to explore the area.	
9	Choose a realistic skill to develop for a year. Work on making something for at least an hour every week.	
10	Assess your progress in Q9 and consider whether you should continue with this craft or choose a new one. Score 10 if you really did make something which you are using now.	
	Remember this assessment is for a very basic level of practical resilience. For the last two tasks, you don't have to become an expert. If you decide to take your craft work further, that's a whole new level. **What you need to understand here is the persistence required to make something by hand, or with simple machinery, and how much skill is required for it to look good. This knowledge is essential in understanding how value and price are related.** How much pollution do you think you generated in making your craft piece?	

	Reskilling Quadrant – Local Materials	Score out of 10
1	Do you use some of your growing space to cultivate scented herbs, such as lavender or roses, for home-made bath products? If this isn't relevant to you, score on finding out about Epsom salts and other proven remedies which can be used in the bath or in skin care.	
2	Gather some materials on a local walk – driftwood, stones, flowers – and explore their qualities. Make some beautiful art. Or not. Don't pick endangered flowers.	
3	Do you value household items for their provenance, for the story which goes with them? Think carefully, score honestly, do better. Next time you go on holiday, buy something useful as a souvenir – a tea-towel, a cup or bowl, a notebook.	
4	Using your chosen craft from the previous section, make a piece including, or inspired by, local materials.	
5	Do you know how your present environment would support your personal survival skills? Have you identified the challenges here?	
6	Have you considered ways in which a small industrial unit could provide helpful tools and facilities in an emergency? Are there any of these in your neighbourhood?	
7	Do you know what strategies could support or revive local production? What would the barriers be?	
8	Do you know the history of your county, its resources, and products? Another double score here, if you've been paying attention!	
9	Can you assess how many of these historical assets are still available? What raw materials could be utilised instead?	
10	Campaign for new housing developments to incorporate small business workshops. Do enough research to join in an informed debate on the issue. Write letters, or comments on planning applications.	
	The production of local resources is essential to resilience. Raw materials can be grown – wool, willow, wood – but without crafters to process these into goods, the economy cannot flow. It's hard to make a living in Britain by selling hand made items. Most crafters have had to give up. Essential skills are lost. **For many people, their main power to influence change is as consumers. If you are prepared to pay the extra for the ultimate in fair trade, we can reverse this process.**	

	Reskilling Quadrant – Local Businesses	**Score out of 10**
1	Do you plan your domestic budget by writing a shopping list every week? This makes it easier to see which items you could source from independent local suppliers.	
2	Do you order anything from a farm shop or box scheme? Buy from a residents' co-op? Research the options you can access here.	
3	Have you explored the options for cleaning products and tried out a good selection of eco-friendly ones? These often use common ingredients and can be made locally.	
4	Do you make your own cakes or other sweet treats? Lose the habit of buying these at a supermarket. You're more in control of what goes into them if you make your own, or go to a family-run bakery.	
5	How often do you drive to an out-of-town supermarket? Aim to cut this down to once a month or less, and only buy heavy or specialist items. Go to a market or farm shop instead. Learning to use stored food helps with this process.	
6	When you need to find nice presents, do you make a point of stocking up in advance at craft events and markets?	
7	Do you plan ahead with larger purchases to explore re-used or locally made options? Remember clothes and shoes are relevant here as well.	
8	Have you studied the manufacturing base of your own country? What products are still made in Britain? Can you source white goods made here? Check the labels on your regular small purchases.	
9	Have you considered how household waste from your area could be turned into raw materials to be used in nearby factories? Glass, cardboard and paper are quite easy to re-use – the process would need a loyal customer base to thrive. How could that work? Do some research.	
10	'Start to step away from the edge one piece of shopping at a time' Score yourself on how important you feel this concept is.	
	Add up your total scores for each action. This will give you a percentage score for this section. **Note some actions you could plan to take, or improve on. Become a retail explorer!**	

Community

In a crisis or emergency, the hundred nearest households to you are the ones you will have to work with. In the old days, this would have been a reasonably sized village, with several pubs, and most of your social life would have been based here too. While not losing sight of the importance of this very local area, today's societies are more thinly spread.

Consider your involvement in your own parish, town or city council area and the adjoining ones as local for the purpose of scoring this section. The closer you can get to home, the better. It's not as achievable as it used to be.

However, any community activity in your wider area could result in your meeting people who live nearby, or inspire you to start something yourself.

Any small organisation, club or society that's used to working together can form the nucleus of a resilience group in an emergency.

Pay attention to the instructions here. The scoring system is slightly different, though the individual score guide is the same:-

- **0** = not done at all / never occurred to me to take an interest
- **1 to 4** = sometimes remember to do this / think about this / know a little bit about it / aware of the issue
- **5 to 8** = working on making a habit here / quite knowledgeable / have done this adventure!
- **9 or 10** = have a useful level of competence and feel that you've got about as far as it's possible to go here, for the time being.

	Community Quadrant – Establishing a Base Line	Score out of 10
1	Can you define the area of your nearest hundred households?	
2	Do you know where your various local authority boundaries are? It's a good exercise to study an Ordnance Survey map and highlight these boundaries. Put the map up on a wall to help familiarise yourself with your local area.	
3	Do you explore the area within walking distance of your home on a regular basis? Take short bus journeys to nearby places of interest?	
4	Do you regularly attend local events, visit independent cafes, restaurants and pubs in your area?	
5	How engaged do you feel with the community within walking distance of your home?	
	Add up your scores for each action here. This will give you a total out of 50. Add this total to the score for each of the Community quadrant sections given below. **For example, if you scored 34 out of 50 in these questions, and 21 out of 50 in the 'Community Projects' section, your total score for 'Community Projects' would be 34+21=55 out of 100, which is 55%** **There are four sections in the Community quadrant. Use these instructions to work out your overall percentage.**	

	Community Quadrant – Community Projects	Score out of 10
1	Have you benefited from a community project – an event, a day out, a facility – in the last year?	
2	Do you know what community projects are going on or being planned in your area?	
3	Have you considered what projects might benefit your area?	
4	Are you currently engaged with a community project? If not, look out for opportunities. Volunteers are often needed for outdoor work, or to help steward an event.	
5	Have you ever organised a local event of some kind? It doesn't matter how small; a micro-sale, a walk in the park, a barbecue, a discussion concerning a local development.	
	How much of this have you covered? Add up your scores for each action. This will give you a total out of 50. **Add it to your base line score to find your percentage in this section.**	

	Community Quadrant – Community Structures	Score out of 10
1	What organisations are active in your area? There will certainly be local authorities who have to meet regularly. What other groups are there?	
2	Do you understand the basic rules and procedures of a community organisation?	
3	Have you thought about local projects which could be started and run if there was an organisation behind them?	
4	Do you belong to any community organisations?	
5	Are you an active member of their management? Score 10 for this question if you are.	
	Add up your scores for each action. This will give you a total out of 50. Add it to your base line score to find your percentage in this section.	

	Community Quadrant - Networking	Score out of 10
1	Do you know what on-line forums and social media are based around your area?	
2	How much do you know about the benefits of networking to an individual? Reading 'Small World' by Mark Buchanan is useful research here.	
3	If you belong to a community organisation which has active links to similar groups nationally, score 10. Groups like the National Trust, the Allotment Society, various sports and games clubs, the Women's Institute and the Rotary Club count here.	
4	Do you feel you have a good local network and can find out what's going on easily? Do you have a good look through any community based news booklets which are delivered, or free to pick up in shops?	
5	Have you attended any local council meetings in the past three months? Make the effort! Score 10 if you are on any of your local councils.	
	Add up your scores for each action. This will give you a total out of 50. Add it to your base line score to find your percentage in this section.	

	Community Quadrant - Fun!	**Score out of 10**
1	Let's be honest here. Going out to a venue owned by a national chain, drinking imported beer and listening to processed music does not count, even if it is within walking distance. Attending a village fete, coffee mornings, a live music performance, a craft, boot or jumble sale does. Locally run entertainment is the criterion here. How close are you to going to something like this every month?	
2	Do you know how to play any card or board games (without having to look up the rules)? Score one for each, up to ten.	
3	Score again for each time you have played one of these in the past month (maximum score is ten!)	
4	Could you plan, or join in with, a small outing somewhere different every month, with friends, family, neighbours, a local club?	
5	Score ten if you did this in the last month	
	Add up your scores for each action. This will give you a total out of 50. Add it to your base line score to find your percentage in this section.	

Emergency Planning

Resilience isn't just about scoring green points. Here comes the wave – learn to ride it!

	Emergency Planning Quadrant – Individual Strategies	Score out of 10
1	Are your phone numbers backed up on paper? Important contact details kept in a notebook can be added to your grab bag. You may not be able to access the Internet, nor keep your phone charged in an emergency, but there could be a land-line available.	
2	A great deal of your personal information is kept in your computer or phone. Do you protect this against your device being lost or broken by using cloud storage? Have you backed up important files, including family photographs, on to a data stick? You could leave a copy of this with a friend for added protection.	
3	Have you a strategy to cope with being locked out of your house?	
4	Do you know how to turn your household utilities off, and how to safely restore services? Have you written the relevant emergency phone numbers in your notebook?	
5	Do you keep a grab bag ready, and check the contents every three months?	
6	Have you a store of tinned and dried foods, water and any medical supplies you may need if you can't leave your house for a few weeks?	
7	Can you remember what LIONEL stands for and how to use it? Score 10 when you don't have to look this up!	
8	Are you familiar with the basic principles of disease prevention and quarantine?	

	Emergency Planning Quadrant – Individual Strategies	Score out of 10
9	If you are out in a storm, or other extreme weather conditions, do you know how to proceed safely, both as a driver and on foot?	
10	Do you have a personal emergency plan? Have you shared this with other people whose help you might require, such as friends, family and neighbours?	
	• **0** = not done at all / never occurred to me to take an interest • **1 to 4** = sometimes remember to do this / think about this / know a little bit about it / aware of the issue • **5 to 8** = working on making a habit here / quite knowledgeable / have done this adventure! • **9 or 10** = have a useful level of competence and feel that you've got about as far as it's possible to go here, for the time being.	

	Emergency Planning Quadrant – Local Strategies	Score out of 10
1	Do you have strategies for maintaining sanitation, drinking water, an energy supply and cooked food in your home in the event of a short disruption of mains services? You need to attend to your own needs before you can be of much use to others.	
2	Could your strategies keep you going for longer? Score 5 if you could last for a week on your own resources; score 10 if you could make it through a fortnight with no mains utilities or opportunities to re-supply. Assume you could refill your water containers at a source less than a mile away.	
3	Do you know how transport and communication in your area might be affected by various types of emergency?	
4	Have you worked out if there could be any changes in your environment - might it become particularly unsafe in places? For example, power lines brought down in a storm might fall into flood water.	
5	Have you considered what resources may be needed in an emergency affecting your immediate community – those nearest 100 households - and how these could be accessed?	
6	Do you know who may need extra help in this small area? Some people could be temporarily vulnerable, such as tourists and the elderly. Where might they be?	
7	What sort of risks does this community of yours face? Are there plans for these at local level? How can you find out?	
8	Have you explored your wider area with a view to identifying resources, skills and useful locations?	
9	Is there a local Community Emergency Group? How much do you know about official response strategies in your county?	
10	How involved with local decision making do you feel? What actions could you take to increase your involvement?	
	Add up your total scores for each action. This will give you a percentage score for this section.	

	Emergency Planning Quadrant – National Plans	Score out of 10
1	Have you studied the official community resilience and emergency planning advice on-line?	
2	Have you looked at your local emergency plan and noted important details? How does it link to national strategies?	
3	Do you know about the roles of the British Red Cross, the Health and Safety Executive, and other Category Two responders?	
4	Do you know enough about useful networks such as RAYNET or 4x4 Response?	
5	How well do you know the paths which the mains services take to your area?	
6	Can you identify several alternative travel routes to key locations in your own life – work, shops, schools?	
7	Do you know your area well enough to draw a rough but accurate map of it? This should certainly cover the 100 households which would form your resilience group – how far outside it are you this familiar with? Could you give directions over the phone to a delivery driver coming from the nearest population centre, or supply depot?	
8	What are the resilient features of your area, and how can you protect these? Are there policies at national level which act against your local resilience? What can you do about this?	
9	Have you attended any local council meetings in the past three months? Include planning and other committees to score this time.	
10	How involved with national decision making do you feel? What actions could you take to increase your involvement?	
	Add up your total scores for each action. This will give you a percentage score for this section. **Calculate your overall practical resilience score using the instructions.** **Now you know your present position and can work to improve it.** **Design and follow a personal Resilience Plan, as described next.**	

Appendix Two

Your Resilience Plan

Any programme of learning has to begin with an assessment of your current knowledge. If you have completed Appendix One, you now possess this.

Study your results. Use a black and white Resilience Wheel template and colour in that fraction of each section which represents your score there. For example, if you got 60% in the Energy section questions, colour in about two-thirds of that on your Wheel.

This exercise helps you to visualise your personal landscape. Which parts are looking good? Which are rather empty?

You'll do better in some sections than others. Design your Resilience Plan to fill these gaps.

Of course, you can work towards practical resilience in any way you like. Anything you do will help the overall level of resilience for everyone. However, if you want to prove your abilities to yourself or to others, you need to work within a framework such as this, which can produce measurable results.

The core level described in the Handbook should be universal. Specialists in any direction can exchange ideas on this common ground. Where individuals are balanced around personal resilience, they appreciate the need for community resilience. Progress is directed towards the common good.

Take a new copy of the black and white Resilience Wheel template, date it, and put it up on your wall. Pay attention to what you do for the next month. Refer to the Handbook and to the questions in Appendix One.

Try to accomplish something new in each section, however small. Colour in the whole of that section when you've done it. At the end of the month, assess how much you've achieved. Which areas were easy to succeed in, and where did you find things difficult?

You can be even more organised and set yourself a list of specific tasks at the start of each month. Large actions can be broken down into several smaller ones. An adventure may take a couple of months to research and plan for. You could learn a single letter of Morse code every week. Your craft projects will move ahead slowly over a whole year.

Persistence in the key. This is where methodical study and keeping records helps. If you keep this up every month, you'll slowly increase your practical resilience with little effort. Tiny actions add up. New habits are often more effective than dramatic change.

At the very least, you should aim to
- be more aware of your mains services and where your food comes from
- buy as much as possible from local independent businesses
- regularly attend nearby community events
- have a grab bag and some basic stores prepared, and keep these maintained

By doing this, you'll be supporting various key initiatives and helping to remove barriers to further resilience. The general knowledge, sustainable practices, community involvement, skills and adventures covered in this Handbook are those which a resilient person ought to possess by default. You may be expert in some already. The goal is to be competent in all.

Once you've completed this course, you'll have a useful level of practical resilience. You should be more confident when dealing with emergencies, better informed and lead a more relaxed and healthy lifestyle.

Appendix Three

Further Progress

As you work through your resilience plan, certain subjects may particularly interest you. If you wish to take these further, more work will be involved. You'll have to choose which parts of the Resilience Wheel to develop, leaving the rest to other people. You all have the shared ground of basic practical resilience for linking up skills and ideas through networking.

For example, I've chosen to explore the **Food** section in the **Resources** quadrant. My resilience garden provides me with a significant amount of food. I wrote 'Recipes for Resilience – Common Sense Cooking for the 21st Century' (2019) based on my work in this section.

I'm also keen to develop **Local Strategies** in the **Emergency Planning** quadrant and joined my parish council, where I advise on these issues. For my chosen craft, I use a technique which I learned on holiday in Turkey to make small rugs from scrap wool.

These activities take up quite a lot of my spare time. I can't do other things, such as create a range of eco-friendly cleaning products or lobby for more cycle paths. I can make sure I attend important local networking events, though. At these, as well as having fun, I meet up with the people and organisations who are working on other aspects of practical resilience. We exchange news and support each others' efforts.

They attend my exhibition on flood prevention; I arrange a hall for a cycle maintenance workshop. Projects and ideas reach a wider audience through the networks described in Chapter 22. Opportunities arise.

It's easier to remember new information and integrate it into your actions if there's a framework for it. The Resilience Wheel provides this. Strategies can be tested against the common principles of practical resilience. Would they further this? Has everything important been considered?

Stay grounded through communicating with your nearest hundred households, other local connections, and knowledge of your own area.

> "Thus the person of devoted character
> Heaps up small things
> In order to achieve something high and great."
> I Ching, Hexagram 46

Recommended Reading

Here's a small selection of important books for the resilience student.

Buchanan, Mark: *Small World,* W W Norton & Company Inc, New York 2002
Dartnell, Lewis: *The Knowledge,* Bodley Head, London 2014
Diamond, Jared: *Collapse; how societies choose to fail or survive,* Allen Lane, London 2005
Fairlie, Simon: *Meat, a Benign Extravagance,* Permanent Publications, Hampshire 2010
Heinberg, Richard: *Powerdown,* Clairview Books, East Sussex 2004
Hodgson, Jacqui and Hopkins, Rob: *Transition in Action — an Energy Descent Action Plan* Transition Town Totnes, Devon 2010
Hopkins, Rob: *The Transition Handbook,* Green Books, Devon 2008
Huxley, Aldous: *Island*
Jensen, Derrick: *Endgame, Volume 1 – The Problem of Civilisation,* Seven Stories Press, New York 2006
Le Guin, Ursula: *Always Coming Home,* Victor Gollancz Ltd, London 1986
Macfadyen, Peter: *Flatpack Democracy – A DIY Guide to Creating Independent Politics,* eco-logic books, 2014
Machiavelli, Niccolo: *The Prince,* (translation) Penguin Books, London 2004
Rowbotham, Michael: *The Grip of Death,* Jon Carpenter Publishing, Oxfordshire 1998
Seymour, John: *The Forgotten Arts and Crafts,* Dorling Kindersley, London 2001 (combined edition)
Stanton, William: *The Rapid Growth of Human Populations 1750 - 2000,* Multi-Science Publishing Company 2003
Walker, Elizabeth J: *Recipes for Resilience – Common Sense Cooking for the 21st Century,* New Generation Publishing 2019

If you're a keen researcher, these books will lead you on to many others

About the Author

Elizabeth J Walker is a teacher and writer with many years of experience in living 'off the grid'.

She gained an Honours degree in Psychology from Edinburgh University in 1977, while restoring an old tenement flat, and rebuilding a car engine to see how it worked. Having failed to prevent the demolition of her street, she bought a camper van and began a career in event management.

With this lifestyle, it was rare to have access to mains services. Water had to be carried from a standing tap, sometimes over a mile away. She used solar panels in the days when you had to solder your own diodes, and cooked with bottled gas.

At the end of the Nineties, Elizabeth moved into a house near Glastonbury, Somerset. There, she began a business in steward training, specialising in off-grid events. She wrote a Steward Handbook and ran large teams of volunteers.

With the introduction of the 2006 Licensing Act, Elizabeth branched out into event welfare work. With industry colleagues she formed a charitable organisation – Medical Welfare – to act as an umbrella group, and worked with emergency services at Silver Command level.

Crisis management at events gave Elizabeth direct experience of how situations can develop and plans must be adapted. She became involved with the local Town Council's emergency planners, where she realised that many of the key elements for a resilient community were not in place.

Working with colleague Linda Benfield, she set about analysing the complex interaction of resources, networks and barriers involved in achieving community resilience. Surrounded by flow charts and spider diagrams, they had a sudden inspiration and reinvented the wheel. Using the Resilience Wheel concept, Elizabeth wrote a training manual for their event volunteers, which evolved into the Resilience books and associated resources.

This second edition of the Handbook, with additional content, was put together with the assistance of Linda Benfield, Josie Pavey and Bethony Walker.

The Resilience Programme outlined here is your opportunity to graduate from passenger to crew.

Lightning Source UK Ltd.
Milton Keynes UK
UKHW030629230420
362136UK00009B/500